W9-DFI-149

What you must see in the
British Isles

What you must see in the
British Isles

Exeter Books • ENIGMA

NEW YORK

Devised by Opus Books
Authors: Jo Darke, Tim Finn
Editor: Elizabeth Longley
Designer: Annie Tomlin

Published and distributed by:
Enigma Books Limited   Exeter Books
58 Old Compton Street   A division of Bookthrift Inc.
London W1V 5PA   New York, New York
IN THE UK, COMMONWEALTH AND   IN THE UNITED STATES OF AMERICA
REST OF THE WORLD, EXCEPT UNITED   ALL RIGHTS RESERVED
STATES OF AMERICA
ISBN 0–85685–939–7   ISBN 0–89673–085–9

Introduction

Exploring a new country can be an unforgettable experience – whether that country is thousands of miles from your homeland, or just on your doorstep. There is an art to being a good traveller however, an art which involves the ability to select the best places to visit with the same unerring confidence with which a gourmet chooses the finest dishes on the menu. *What you must see in the British Isles* encapsulates these qualities of taste and discrimination perfectly. Britain has such a myriad range of attractions that it would literally take years to discover them on your own.

This beautifully illustrated book is a connoisseur's guide to around eighty key places to see in England, Scotland, Wales and Ireland. They all have unique characteristics of their own of course – the Georgian splendours of Bath are unrivalled, and there is no other shopping precinct like the Rows in Chester to be found anywhere; natural landscapes like the Scottish Highlands and the Lake District are not only beautiful in themselves, they also enshrine the work of some of the nation's finest poets. Each cathedral, castle, abbey, church, village and street has its own story to tell, in architecture and history. Other facets of Britain are expressed too – the classic vulgarity of breezy Blackpool is as typically British as Buckingham Palace or the Tower of London. Added together, all these places provide a balanced guide to the British Isles in all their rich variety.

Individual entries are compact and precise, packed with information and illustrated with stunning photographs, many in full colour. There are five sections, each alphabetically arranged, covering England, Wales, Scotland and Ireland, plus a separate section for London. For practical information on how to get there there is a useful map at the end of the book, also a detailed directory supplying the latest addresses and telephone numbers for the specific places described, and details of the major tourist boards. *What you must see in the British Isles* is an invaluable handbook for the casual tourist and the determined explorer, and a handsome souvenir for fireside browsing.

England and Wales

London

Ireland

Scotland

England and
Wales

Skiddaw (3054ft) is one of four Cumbrian peaks exceeding 3000ft in England's magnificent Lake District.

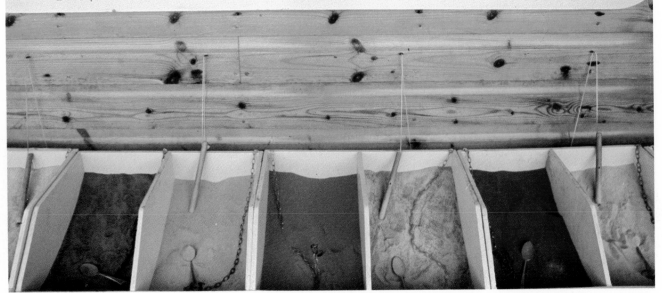

Alum Bay and the Needles

The stark chalk pinnacles known as the Needles are remnants of a ridge, now covered by the sea, that once joined the Purbeck Downs in Dorset to the Freshwater Peninsula at the western tip of the Isle of Wight. Along the north edge of the peninsula are the multi-coloured cliffs of Alum Bay, layers of brown, pink and yellow sandstone that have been pushed and twisted into their present formation by primeval upheavals underground.

Tennyson lived at Farringford among the quiet downland farms of the Freshwater Peninsula, now owned by the National Trust. The small villages and farms were mostly inhabited by native islanders, 'corkheads'. The 'overners', who inhabit the rest of the island, were migrants from the mainland. Tennyson took daily walks to look out over the Needles, crossing High Down to take in the air, which he said was 'worth 6d a pint'.

The Victorians' affection for the island's chalk downs and chines established a rewarding trade in tourism that remains to this day. Much of the unploughed chalk down is covered with short grass and flowers, as well as gorse and hawthorn. The rich and varied flora is of particular interest to botanists. Compton Beaches is a popular resort for families and is excellent for sea bathing. Hundreds of visitors follow Tennyson's path over what is now Tennyson's Down, or ride down to the beach from the clifftop on Alum's alpine-style chairlift. But the stark white pinnacles standing out of blue or grey seas are landmarks for Channel sea traffic, and the rock formation in Alum Bay is a continual source of fascination for visiting geologists.

Arundel Castle

The castle stands guard over the town of Arundel and over the river, meadows and woods of the Arun Valley. Roger de Montgomery started the inner gateway in about 1086, soon after the Conquest, and since then the castle has been extended, besieged, rebuilt, neglected and magnificently restored. Today, the home of the Duke of Norfolk, it is a Victorian Gothic masterpiece. The castle, and the surrounding acres of parkland, are open to the public at advertised times.

The grand interior has a vast baronial

ALUM BAY, ISLE OF WIGHT
Above: Formed over 50 million years ago, the cliffs of Alum Bay contain some 12 distinct shades of sandstone. The variegated colours are particularly beautiful after rain.
Right: Alum Bay at sunset. The Isle of Wight is still relatively unspoilt, although resorts such as Ryde, Sandown, Shanklin and Ventnor are crowded in summer months.

ARUNDEL CASTLE
Overleaf: Although its origins date from the time of the Conquest, Arundel Castle was constructed mainly in the nineteenth century and is a splendid example of Victorian Gothic. The original structure, of which the shell keep remains, was badly damaged during the Civil War.

hall supported by beams cut from oaks in the park. The early nineteenth century library is built of British Honduras mahogany, and the picture gallery running the entire width of the castle is lined with pictures of the Dukes of Norfolk and the Earls of Arundel which reach back over 500 years. These and other rooms hold a treasury of period furniture, paintings and tapestries.

The town, mostly of Victorian houses, climbs steeply up from the river to the castle and park. The fourteenth century Fitzalan Chapel, entered from the park, adjoins Arundel's parish church of St Nicholas which is entered from the town. The Anglican church and the Roman Catholic chapel are separated by a medieval ironwork screen, backed with glass. Farther along the street a huge Roman Catholic Cathedral, built by the 15th Duke in 1868, adds to the grandeur of this Sussex town.

Bath Spa

A Roman watering place lies beneath the most complete and the best preserved Georgian city in England. Bath, sheltered by seven hills, is watered by the River Avon and endowed with hot springs flowing in from the Mendips. The springs were known to the Romans, who settled here around A.D. 44. They built a city and elaborate baths with fountains, sacrificial altars and memorials. These they dedicated to the part-Celtic part-Roman Goddess, Sul Minerva. They called the settlement Aquae Sulis.

Much of the Roman life-style can be seen from the great baths in the centre of the city, which were uncovered in 1878 by the city engineer. In restoring them the Victorians dallied with the idea of covering them over in iron and glass, but they remain open to the sky, colonnaded in Roman style. Some of the paving is original, as is the lead flooring of the baths. The lead was mined locally by the Romans. Bath stone was a major export and the Roman city grew to be an important centre.

The baths formed a complex of treatment areas which can be traced today through rooms such as the Laconicum, the Caldarium or the Tepidarium. Waters from the central reservoir gush from a culvert in the wall called the steaming spring, and another stone culvert, built to carry waste water, is still used for that purpose. In the site museum, fragments and jewellery from the Temple of Sul Minerva and from other nearby excavations, as well as from the baths, form among the best-preserved Roman relics in the country. A gilded bronze head of Minerva is considered one of our greatest national treasures. Much more is known to lie beneath Bath's Georgian streets.

Bath's modern reputation is based on its revival as a spa in the eighteenth century and on its Georgian architectural achievements. Its bridges, crescents and squares date from that time, which coincided with the arrival of the socialite and dandy Beau Nash from London. With him came the fashionable elite, and Bath became an elegant watering place. Meanwhile, Ralph Allen, a wealthy quarry owner, went into collaboration with the architect John Wood. Throughout the century the mellow Bath stone was used to create Queen's Square and the Circus, John Wood the Younger's superb Royal Crescent, Robert Adam's Pulteney Bridge, supporting houses and shops, and the unrivalled elegance of Great Pulteney Street, by Thomas Baldwin. In 1796 the Pump Room, later to adjoin the Roman baths, was built near the Abbey to make the most of the warm water gushing at the rate of 8000 gallons per hour from springs probably a mile deep.

Blackpool

Blackpool, England's best known pleasure resort, has seven miles of promenade, seafront tram rides and three piers. The Blackpool Tower, constructed in 1891, takes visitors 518 feet up for breathtaking views over the seafront, where the Golden Mile offers fun-fair amusements, Bingo, donkey rides, kiss-me-quicks, candy floss and Blackpool rock. Within the tower itself are a zoo, an aquarium, a circus, and a ballroom with the great Blackpool organ. During September and October the Blackpool Illuminations make a marvellous spectacle with the tower picked out in lights and the promenades lit below.

Behind the seafront are terraces of smartly painted Victorian houses, with traditional seaside landladies offering family accommodation. Since the time of the Industrial Revolution when holiday-makers stayed in farms, cottages and barns, until now when Lancashire's mills and factories close for the annual holidays called 'wakes', Blackpool has been the favourite resort. Traditionally, families save throughout the year so that the amusements can be enjoyed without stint.

BATH
The Great Bath, built after A.D. 44, is one of several built by the Romans in the town they called Aquae Sulis. The therapeutic qualities of its water brought the town renewed prosperity in the eighteenth century, when it became the most fashionable watering place in England. Today it is most famed for its elegant and well-preserved buildings— built in the same golden stone as the Roman baths.

BE
L

10
STORES

8 GAL. KEG
MILLER L

17

Greenwich Time 100 years old

GREENWICH, England (UPI) — Greenwich Mean Time has celebrated its 100th anniversary at zero longitude.

Since 1884, a brass strip in the ground outside a domed 17th century observatory on the Thames, two miles downstream from the Tower of London, has marked the line from which the world's time is calculated.

The "O" meridian line marked by the strip runs around the world, north and south through the poles. When the sun is directly overhead, all areas to the west of the strip are before noon and those east are afternoon.

Free-falling parachutists and the Duke of Edinburgh took part in Tuesday's ceremonies.

The anniversary actually will be in October, but was celebrated in June in order to assure fairer weather.

An international conference in Washington on Oct. 13, 1884, decided "to adopt the meridian passing through the center of the transit instrument at the Observatory of Greenwich as the initial meridian for longitude." Greenwich Mean Time, or GMT, was born.

Tuesday, precise time signals piped daily from outside the Greenwich observatory — now the National Maritime Museum — aid navigators at sea and aircraft pilots in reckoning their positions.

ROYAL PAVILION, BRIGHTON
Overleaf: In this Oriental fantasy, designed mainly by John Nash, the Prince Regent indulged his taste for opulent living. A mixture of Chinese and Indian styles, it employed the latest technology. The domes and minarets were made of cast iron, as were the 'bamboo' staircases. The building was one of the first in the world to be lit by gas, and it was centrally heated throughout.

ROYAL CRESCENT, BRIGHTON
Right: Another popular seaside resort—but one with an elegant Regency aspect— Brighton is only about an hour by train from London. Originally a sleepy fishing village called Brighthelmstone, it became fashionable in the late 1700s when the Prince Regent (later George IV) took up residence there to escape the constraints of life at Court.

BLACKPOOL BEACH
Left: Sea bathing and seaside entertainments on a lavish scale attract eight million visitors to Blackpool each year, chiefly from the Midlands and the North. In recent years it has taken on new significance as the venue of political party conferences.

There are quieter pleasures to be found in Blackpool's gardens and parks, playgrounds, golf courses and bowling greens. Stanley Park has a boating lake, rose gardens and a conservatory, as well as Italianate gardens, bowls, tennis and golf. In the town there are several theatres and a waxworks, and in Queen Street the Grundy Galleries contain a permanent collection of nineteenth and twentieth century British art. But Blackpool's main purpose and pleasure is the purveyance of fun.

The Royal Pavilion, Brighton

The early years of the Pavilion saw Brighthelmstone's transformation from fishing village fallen on hard times (much of it swept away in 1703 and 1705

by savage storms) to the fashionable, raffish, Royal resort of Brighton with its racecourse, piers and Regency parades. Today, with a magnificent modern marina recently completed, it is still 'Queen of the South'.

In 1750 Dr Richard Russell of Lewes published his paper urging the health-giving properties of seawater; thereafter Prince George became a regular visitor to Brighton. In 1787 'Prinny's Pleasure Dome' was built by Henry Holland to a classical design, and named the Marine Pavilion. Twenty years later the Pavilion was enlarged and given an exotic Chinese interior. William Porden added stables and the riding house, and the oriental aspect of his designs prompted the Prince to modify the rest of the Pavilion. John Nash won the commission and

today's rich confection of minaret and dome is his.

Nash's Pavilion aroused much disapproval; Sidney Smith commented that the dome of St Paul's had 'come down and pupped'. Despite the jibes, the Prince continued to visit Brighton whilst he was Regent and then King and enjoyed his 'Pleasure Dome' to the full. His brother William IV used the Pavilion, and so did Queen Victoria, who disliked it. She disposed of most of the furnishing and left the Pavilion to moulder while the rest of Brighton continued to prosper – helped by the railway, built from London to Brighton in 1841, which truly made Brighton 'London by the Sea'.

In 1850 the Pavilion, stripped of its contents, was sold to the Brighton Corporation for £50,000. One hundred years later, the Corporation effected a magnificent restoration for the Festival of Britain. Buckingham Palace and Windsor Castle returned much of the original furnishing, and other treasures were tracked down in antique shops. Today Prinny's Pleasure Dome, amid its palm trees and lawns, beside the health-giving sea, is open for the pleasure of all.

Canterbury Cathedral

Spiritually the heart of England, seat of the Anglican Church and of the Prelates, Canterbury Cathedral occupies the site of the vanished cathedral built when St Augustine arrived on a mission from Rome in A.D. 597. Set down within the ancient walls of Canterbury, its towers soar over old streets, modern developments, gardens and parks. The town gathered around it stands on the ground of Roman Durovernum, City of the Marsh, then, and now, on the route from the south-east port cities of Kent to London.

The architecture of today's Cathedral spans eight centuries, from Norman to Victorian Gothic. The Norman beginnings can be seen in the vast crypt, the largest in Britain, with its fancifully adorned Romanesque columns, where in the north-west corner Thomas Becket was slain in 1170. A fire destroyed the Norman choir in 1174, which was soon after rebuilt with donations from pilgrims who had come to visit Becket's shrine. Trinity Chapel was built on the site of the shrine, and a circular annexe was made for the medieval throne of Purbeck marble, St Augustine's chair, on which archbishops are crowned. On the south side of Trinity Chapel visitors can see the impressive tomb of Edward the Black Prince who was buried here in 1376. On the north side are the tombs of Henry IV and his Queen, Joan of Navarre, their effigies carved in alabaster. The rich windows depicting miracles and cures are thirteenth century; Henry Yevele built the nave, and in the fifteenth century the fine Bell Harry Tower was added. In 1840 William the Conqueror's north-west tower was replaced in Gothic form.

Outside Canterbury's walls are the ruins of St Augustine's Abbey, used through the centuries as a place of worship, a palace and, in the last century, a brewery. Its crumbled walls are of Saxon and Norman origin. Close to this important site is St Martin's, the oldest of England's churches still in use. It is thought the pagan King Ethelbert's wife, Bertha, worshipped here before St Augustine landed in A.D. 597. By then the King was ripe for conversion, and St Augustine baptized him at St Martin's font.

Cheddar Gorge

Cheddar Gorge is one of Britain's most spectacular natural landmarks. The 450-foot cliffs and the series of caverns, or 'holes', were cut in the geological past by rivers wearing down the soft limestone of the Mendip Hills. The Gorge itself was once a cave, until the covering rock collapsed. Stone Age men lived in the caves. Tools, weapons and a skeleton are exhibited in a museum opposite Gough's Cave. Weird, wonderful stalactites and stalagmites create a kaleidoscope of colour in the two main caves, Gough's and Cox's, which are open all the year round. The most dramatic views are at the north end of the Gorge reached by 'Jacob's Ladder', 355 steps cut into the side of the cliff. Through the trees and grasses the cars look like beetles on the road below.

At the south end of the Gorge is the Cheddar Motor Museum, and farther on is the village of Cheddar whose inhabitants make the famous cheese to a special recipe, as a cottage industry, to supplement that produced from the one cheddar cheese 'factory'. Another rarity is the Cheddar Pink, an exquisite, scented carnation so popular with the souvenir-mad Victorians that it is now almost extinct. Cheddar's limestone and climate provide the only conditions where this delicate, fragrant flower can grow wild.

CANTERBURY CATHEDRAL
The mother church of the Anglican faith, Canterbury Cathedral dates from the eleventh century, although much of the present building was constructed later. The result is a building of great architectural richness, which also contains some of the finest medieval stained glass remaining in England. During the Middle Ages Canterbury attracted pilgrims from all over Europe, who came to pray at the shrine of St. Thomas Becket.

DARTMOOR
Overleaf: Although most of Dartmoor has a wild, wind-swept look, the area is dotted with villages and hamlets, inhabited mainly by farmers whose cattle and sheep graze the surrounding moors. Archaeological remains suggest that people were living on Dartmoor during the Mesolithic period (15,000 to 3500 B.C.), and there is ample evidence of a thriving Bronze Age culture in the region.

CHEDDAR GORGE
Left: The stalagmites and stalactites of Gough's Cave. This cave and Cox's are the most famous of the more than 400 caves and holes in the area. The bones of prehistoric men, who may have been cannibals, were found in some of the caves; in others, Roman coins have been discovered. In the nearby village of Cheddar visitors can see a fine fourteenth-to-fifteenth century church and market cross.

Chester: The Rows

No other shopping precinct like the Rows exists in England. They are perhaps the most distinctive feature of Chester, a city particularly noted for its archaeological and architectural wealth. These medieval half-timbered buildings are on two levels. Above the pavement and shops at street level are more shops, which are approached from a continuous covered gallery. Paved and wooden balustraded steps lead to the upper balcony from the street. Below ground level there are vaulted cellars. One such cellar, at 39 Bridge Street, has a bath cut out of the rock with a Roman furnace for heating it.

The Rows occupy both sides of three of Chester's main streets, Eastgate,

Watergate and Bridge Street. Rows on the west side of the fourth, Northgate Street, were demolished in the seventeenth century. Records show that the Rows existed in the early fourteenth century, but they were probably in use even before then. There are also some exceptionally fine Tudor houses. Of greatest interest are Bishop Lloyd's House, Stanley Place and Leche House.

As an example of a medieval walled city, Chester is unique in Britain. Nowhere else are there such well preserved ramparts. These, which extend in a two and a half mile circuit, have Roman, Saxon and Norman foundations, but many of the towers and gates were added in the Middle Ages. The view from these fortified walls, which the visitor can walk around, gives a fairly accurate

THE ROWS, CHESTER
Right: These distinctive half-timbered buildings house two levels of shops and are unique of their type in England. Another feature of Chester is its well-preserved city wall.

representation of what a medieval walled town must have been like.

Chester has had a long and varied history. It was once a Roman fort, later it was virtually destroyed by Saxon invaders and in Norman times it was a prosperous trading post. From King Charles's Tower, Charles I is said to have witnessed the disastrous battle of Rowton Moor (1645). After protracted seige Chester was finally starved into submission by the Roundheads. The Tower now houses a Civil War exhibition.

Of additional interest to the visitor are Abbey Square, where the Chester Mystery plays were performed in medieval times, the Cathedral, mainly Norman with later additions, the Church of St John the Baptist, a large and imposing Norman building, and the Grosvenor Museum, which houses most of Chester's Roman remains.

Dartmoor

Devon's Dartmoor, the largest area of open country in southern England, is one of the wildest and most desolate tracts in Britain. Volcanic upheavals 400 million years ago formed Dartmoor, a lonely stretch of peat, bog, and granite tor, which receives much rain and is the source of numerous streams. The small shaggy ponies running wild over the land are descended from the breed that pulled Boadicea's war chariots. There are 365 square miles of National Park, with areas given over to the British Army for training, parts taken for reservoirs, and some acres planted with pine. Yes Tor reaches 2028 feet and High Willhayes 2039 feet to make Dartmoor England's highest stretch south of the Lakes. In the Bronze Age, this treeless waste was dry enough for people to settle above surrounding lowland swamps. Traces of prehistoric farms remain – pounds, hut circles of granite, and burial mounds.

Climatic changes brought the rain and Dartmoor was sparsely populated until the twelfth century, when the discovery of tin established a mining industry. For a while, mining brought power. 'Stannary' (derived from the Latin word for 'tin') towns were set up near the moor and across the border in Cornwall, where tin was also mined. Stannary courts upheld their own laws and regulated price and weight of the ore. The fourteenth century saw mining decline and the Black Death ravage the district.

Today there are isolated smallholdings where the land will support sheep. Around the edges of the moor are villages with thatched cottages, watered by rushing streams. At Dartmeet and Postbridge there are clapper bridges, made from single vast slabs of granite, some supported by dry-stone columns mid-stream. They were built for horses and carts in the mining era. Near Chagford, which was once a Stannary town, there is one of Dartmoor's finest pre-Christian stone circles. There are Bronze Age barrows west of Hamel Down near the village of Widecombe-in-the-Moor where the church, 'the cathedral in the moor', with its pinnacled tower, was built in 1500, a symbol of the miners' prosperity. Widecombe Fair, which takes place in September, is well-known from the plight of the hapless group 'Old Uncle Tom Cobleigh and all' who, in the traditional song, borrowed Tom Pearce's grey mare to go to the fair and did not return home. Princetown, surrounded by equally intractable moorland, is the location of Dartmoor Prison built from 1806 to 1813 when the Lord Warden of the Stannaries, Sir Thomas Tyrwhitt, engaged French prisoners from the Napoleonic Wars to work on his grand house, Tor Royal, half a mile away on the moor.

Dartmoor's chief attraction, a kind of haunted loneliness, is best appreciated by walking. Before starting it is advisable to consult locally, since mists can materialize, swirling and treacherous, from out of a clear blue sky. Various books are available which give directions away from bogs, to prehistoric sites and scenic treks. The Post Office will advise about weather conditions and about the Army's shooting programme – red flags are shown in areas where gunnery practice is taking place.

Fishbourne Roman Palace

This outstanding Roman palace, built between A.D. 71 and 80, is partly covered by the village of Fishbourne and the Portsmouth road. The palace, with its near-perfect mosaics, has provided enough evidence in fragments and remains for experts to say that this was probably the residence of the British-born ruler Cogidubnus, whom the Romans put in charge of Chichester.

Open to the public, but sheltered by twentieth century glass and pine, is the residential north wing. Visitors can walk on raised platforms to see the rich mosaic flooring, the most memorable of Fishbourne's features, and all that remains in any completeness since the building was burned to the ground in

FLATFORD MILL
Overleaf: Flatford Mill is deep in the heart of Constable country. From the mills at Flatford and Dedham, Constable's father, a wealthy miller, sent the flour by barge to Mistely to be carried in his own sailing ship to London. Flatford Mill was built in the 1730s on the site of former mills dating back to Domesday. A painting of the mill by Constable hangs in the Tate Gallery in London.

A.D. 280, about 200 years after it was begun. One panel, roughly 17 feet square and surrounded by a decorative border, shows on a central medallion a winged boy on a dolphin. Nearby semi-circles depict sea horses and sea panthers.

Through the once-porticoed south entrance to this wing is a formal garden laid out with box hedges, roses and acanthus; all plants that would be found in a Roman garden. The original plan can still be detected, and pipes have been found that may have fed fountains. Indoors are hypocausts for underfloor heating and hot baths.

The north wing and the garden are all that can be uncovered. To the east and west of the garden, formerly graced with columns, lie the administrative quarters of the palace. The south wing, the King's residential quarter, completes the quad-

rangle. Palace and ground covered an estimated 10 acres. The site was discovered in 1960 but eight years elapsed before archaeologists, artists, scientists and historians, uncovering floors, masonry, pottery and coins, reconstituted the garden and set up the site museum.

Flatford Mill

Flatford Mill on the River Stour, was one of the eighteenth century water mills owned by the father of the landscape painter, John Constable. It was immortalized by the painter along with much of the surrounding countryside: 'These scenes made me a painter . . . as long as I am able to hold a brush, I shall never cease to paint them'. A path approaching the mill and its timbered houses, the

FISHBOURNE ROMAN PALACE
Right: The superb mosaics are the featured attraction at Fishbourne. Naturalistic and geometric motifs are combined with great sophistication, showing the skill of Roman craftsmen as well as the high status of the owner, who may have been the governor of Chichester.

white cottage of Willy Loft and riverside trees leads from the village of East Bergholt, where the painter was born.

Constable's father, a wealthy miller, discouraged painting as a profession and the young man, working at the family mill for a year, became known as 'the handsome miller'. But the urge to paint and encouragement from a friend of his father's took him to London, where in 1799 he entered the Royal Academy School. Constable's knowledge of the Suffolk countryside brought a realism to his work which was a departure from the fashionable stylized work of Claude and other Arcadian painters whom Constable admired, but had no inclination to emulate.

The painter lived in London but made long visits to Suffolk. His first major work, *Dedham Vale*, completed when he was 35, shows the location of his father's other mill at Dedham. The mill at Flatford where Constable spent much of his boyhood remains unaltered, and is now used by the Council for the Promotion of Field Studies, under the protection of the National Trust. There are amenities for visitors near by and in the summer the lanes are crowded with traffic. Unchanged, however, are the water meadows and mills and the glowing golden light of Suffolk which pervade so much of Constable's work.

Hampton Court Palace

This magnificent palace was given to Henry VIII in 1526 by Cardinal Wolsey 15 years after it was built, in an attempt to keep the King's favour. In those days it was reached by barge from Westminster along the River Thames.

Today, four hours from Westminster, the boat arrives at this unmistakably Tudor palace with its characteristic diamond patterned red-brick walls, its chimneys, vast stretches of lawn and avenues of trees. Henry VIII built the Great Hall, the hammer-beam roof and the tennis court, and added the astronomical clock which crowns Anne Boleyn's Gatehouse. It was one of his favourite palaces. Here he played Royal Tennis in the closed court, jousted on the green sward and was married to his last wife, Catherine Parr. Five of his wives lived at Hampton Court and two, Catherine Howard and Jane Seymour, reputedly haunt the palace to this day.

Sir Christopher Wren built the south and east wings of the palace for William III in 1689, and designed the Fountain Court and the Orangery. The gardens were redesigned at the same time by George London and Henry Wise, who added the Fountain Garden and the famous maze.

The palace contains a collection of furniture, clocks and tapestries and among the superb paintings are works by Holbein, Titian, Veronese, Correggio and Tintoretto. Henry VIII's weapons can be seen in the Guardroom.

The knot garden is aromatic with varieties of herbs and, in season, purple grapes gleam on the Great Vine which was planted in 1769.

Kew Gardens

The Royal Botanical Gardens at Kew are the world's most famous botanical gardens. They are the location of a training centre for botanists and gardeners, a quarantine station for plants in transit between different countries, a major centre for the classification and identification of plants, and a world distribution centre for plants and plant matter and for botanical information. They were laid out in the eighteenth century for Princess Augusta, mother of George III, on the site of two royal palaces along the bank of the Thames. As well as containing a vast collection of the world's flora, Kew Gardens is also one of the most beautiful parks in the world.

The centrepiece for visitors is Decimus Burton's Palm House, one of the first wrought iron and glass structures, built between 1844 and 1848. It is approached along the Broad Walk from the main gates between clumps of Turkey Oak, Japanese Cherries and Weeping Beech. Inside, apart from palms of almost every known variety, are bread-fruit, balsa, bamboo, banana and other tropical plants. An iron spiral staircase leads to a gallery about 30 feet above the floor.

The Palm House backs on to a rose garden and it faces a large ornamental pond with weeping willows, and with fountains at the far end. Bread can be thrown for huge goldfish to catch above the water. To the north of the pond, near the grand main gates, also Decimus Burton's ironwork, are clusters of greenhouses sheltering succulents, cacti, filmy fern and other exotics.

The gardens are laid out so that woodland, groves, and avenues of trees are on the west side bounded by the river, with lawns, gardens and hot-houses primarily to the east. Near the centre of the gardens is a large lake with alder, spruce and redwood along its south shore. A number of Classical temples intended as rest posts remain from Princess Augusta's day, and it was for the Princess that William Chambers also designed the Japanese Gateway and the Chinese Pagoda. The first stands near Mosque Hill just west of the Pagoda, and is a scaled-down copy of a Buddhist temple. The decorative pagoda, in the south-east corner of the gardens, is 163 feet high. It ascends in ten storeys of diminishing diameter, and contains a staircase.

Other reminders of the Hanoverians are the Queen's Cottage, in the south, and Kew Palace which is close to the river in the north-west of the gardens. The Cottage was designed as a rustic summer-house, and its bluebell woods are much visited in the spring. Kew Palace is furnished as it was when George III and his family used it as a country retreat. It is of pretty red brick with tall chimneys and ornamental gables, and was built in 1631 by Samuel Fortrey, the son of a Dutch refugee. Behind it is the Queen's Garden, laid out out as a seventeenth century garden in 1969.

For wet weather there are some interesting museums. The Marianne North Gallery, facing the Temperate House from the south-east wall, houses many paintings of plants by this nineteenth century artist. The General Museum faces the Palm House Pond, and among its exhibits is a 4000 year old Egyptian boomerang. The Wood Museum is among the cluster of nurseries, laboratories and administrative buildings by the main gate.

Outside the main gate, on the north side of Kew Green, the Herbarium and Library are open to students. The Herbarium has a collection of seven million dried plants, thought to be the largest such collection in the world.

The Lake District

The Cumbrian mountains and their lakes encompass 886 square miles of National Park, justly designated as an area of outstanding natural beauty. Nowhere in England is there such a variety of magnificent scenery as in the Lake District with its 16 principal lakes, 22 passes, and 179 peaks attaining more than 2000 feet. The mountains are bounded on the north by the Solway Firth and on the south by Morecambe Bay. Flat silver and green turfy shoreline, red headlands and old coal ports form the strip of coast between. To the east of the Lake District is the Vale of Eden and the backbone of England, the Pennine Chain.

The action of Ice Age glaciers upon rocks previously subjected to millennia of successive arching, compressing, eruption, silting and sinking, has created within the region a broad diversity of 'natural beauty' varying from the savagely spectacular to the serene. A high annual rainfall gives the air a soft clarity. The small, deep corries in scoops of rock, like Small Water which is close to the reservoir, Hawes Water, reflect the dense blue or cold grey of the sky. Long, low waters like Windermere ripple with the greens and browns of grass. The heights are unremarkable by global standards for Scafell Pike at 3210 feet is England's loftiest peak; but they create their own majesty. The lakes beneath are long and narrow, radiating along the lines of the ranges like the spokes of a wheel with Thirlmere near the hub.

Windermere, England's largest lake, stretches north towards Thirlmere from the southern boundary of the Lake District. Today it is a pleasure resort, offering every diversion from water skiing to bowls in surroundings of supreme beauty. The mountains are not close and the shores are gently wooded slopes. Bowness and Windermere are reached by train and the lake can be approached from the motorway. A main road runs north-south along the gentle eastern shore past the resorts to fork north-west for Ambleside, or to follow the wild valley of Troutbeck into Wansfell, thence over the Kirkstone Pass.

The Troutbeck road falls steeply to the pastoral village of Patterdale, on the shores of Ullswater, near whose shores Wordsworth saw the daffodils which inspired his best known poem. Ullswater, seven miles long and smaller only than Windermere, turns from north to north-west towards the Vale of Eden and the ancient town of Penrith, at the north-east limits of the region. Ullswater's twisting shape creates crosswinds, a challenge for yachtsmen, but the sails and the serene waters make a lyrical foil for the lofty crags around. Visitors can take motor boat excursions, from Glenridding to the beautiful Pooley Bridge, the length of the lake.

The road turning towards Ambleside along the northern, more mountainous end of Windermere, penetrates the region associated with the Lake poets, Wordsworth, Southey and Coleridge, and the coterie of writers who visited the

CRUMMOCK WATER
Overleaf: One of the most unspoiled parts of the Lake District, Crummock is owned by the National Trust, which also owns nearby Buttermere. Trout fishing (by permission) is one of its attractions.

KEW GARDENS
Landscaped by Capability Brown in the eighteenth century, the 300 acres of Kew Gardens contain many exotic varieties of plant as well as those native to Britain. The Gardens also include several reminders of the Hanoverian royal house, such as a Chinese pagoda built for Princess Augusta, mother of George III, the picturesque Queen's Cottage, and Kew Palace, a favourite retreat of George III and his large family. Since 1841 the Gardens have been a national property, dedicated to the study and cultivation of plants.

Lake District when William and Dorothy Wordsworth lived at Grasmere. Visitors can see portraits of Wordsworth and some of his manuscripts at Dove Cottage, overlooking Grasmere, backed by Helm Crag and Nab Scar, where the Wordsworths lived from 1799 until 1808. There is peaceful walking country around Grasmere and Rydal Water, the small, beautiful lake beneath Rydal Fell. Here Wordsworth lived from 1813 (becoming Poet Laureate in 1843) until his death in 1850. The slopes of Wansfell, the wooded river valleys and the views over Rydal Water remind us that the poets were perhaps drawn here by the lakes' own poetry.

Throughout the region are small cottages, churches and towns which resound with Victorian literary names. At Ambleside, between Windermere and Rydal, on the slopes of Wansfell, the writer Harriet Martineau entertained George Eliot and Charlotte Brontë. Memorial windows to Wordsworth are found in the church, which was designed in 1854 by Gilbert Scott, and there is a Ruskin library. These old towns are centres for climbing, sightseeing and boating, but they also retain the customs of earlier times when the region was more remote and the towns were only visited by farmers on market days. Ambleside's sheepdog trials in August are internationally known, and in July a rush-bearing ceremony is enacted. This procession of children with crosses of rushes and flowers is a survival of the custom of strewing rushes or hay on the floor before the days of carpets. Grasmere also has a rush-bearing ceremony; and in August the Grasmere sports attract huge crowds to watch Cumberland and Westmorland wrestling, and races to the top of Grey Crag.

From there the road leads north through the centre of the Lakes between Thirlmere and the lofty ridge of Helvellyn. Thirlmere is a spruce lined, narrow strip running along the foot of Helvellyn, whose flooding in the late nineteenth century to make a reservoir, caused the furore that helped to found the National Trust in 1895. (The Trust now owns more than an eighth of the Lakes' National Park.) North of Thirlmere across Castlerigg is Keswick, situated in meadows below Saddleback and Skiddaw, on the north-west shore of Derwentwater, 'the Queen of English lakes'. Keswick, too, is one of the loveliest Lake towns. The poets Coleridge, Southey and Shelley all lived here at one time, and their manuscripts are displayed at the Fitzpark Museum, while Turner's paintings and one by Ruskin are in the Art Gallery.

Derwentwater and Bassenthwaite, linked by the Derwent, form the north-west line of the lakes. Bassenthwaite is an excellent perch-fishing lake between Skiddaw on the east and Lord's Seat on the west. The River Derwent can be followed by road from the south end of Derwentwater through the spectacular 'beauty, horror and immensity' of the Jaws of Borrowdale. Seathwaite, the village at the end of the minor road, is surrounded by wild high peaks.

From Keswick along Borrowdale, one can turn west at the fork for Seathwaite and then around the Buttermere Fells to Buttermere Lake. This runs north-west through meadows and woods to Crummock Water, and the western edge of the Lakes. There are mountains on three sides of Buttermere and pastures of grazing cattle, whence Buttermere got its name. On the southern and northern shores there are pleasant climbs and walks, and boats can be hired for fishing. Scale Force, a spectacular waterfall over a drop of 100 feet is best seen after heavy rain. This is perhaps the most tranquil of all the lakes.

Leeds Castle

This impressive medieval fortress is surrounded by a moat on which glide black swans, stately as Leeds' historic walls. The first castle, begun in A.D. 857 by Ledian, chief minister of the King of Kent, was a wooden structure built on an island formed by damming the River Len. William the Conqueror gave the castle to a cousin, Hamon de Crevecoeur, and in 1119 Robert de Crevecoeur rebuilt the castle in stone as a country retreat. Edward I strengthened the defences and gave it to Eleanor of Castile, then to his second wife Margaret of France. Leeds became known as the Lady's Castle, to be granted as a dower to medieval queens.

Edward II presented the castle to Lord Badlesmere and in 1321 Badlesmere's bailiff, acting on orders, refused to admit Queen Isabella ('She-Wolf of France') who sought shelter there. Edward II stormed the castle: Badlesmere was beheaded at Canterbury and his bailiff, Colpeper, was hanged at Leeds' gates. The She-Wolf held the castle until her death in 1358.

Among other resident queens was Edward III's Philippa of Hainault, Richard II's Anne of Bohemia and

LEEDS CASTLE
This majestic medieval castle, set in grounds landscaped in the eighteenth century by Capability Brown, was the home of many of England's queens. Among them was the unhappy Catherine of Aragon, first wife of Henry VIII, who lived here for many years. Her daughter, Mary I, confined her half-sister, later Elizabeth I, to the castle, fearing her popularity with the English people. A pair of pink shoes that belonged to Elizabeth's mother, Anne Boleyn, are on display in the castle.

Henry IV's Joan of Navarre who spent a summer there to avoid the plague raging in London. Catherine de Valois, widow of Henry V, fell in love with her Clerk of the Wardrobe – the Anglesey squire Owen Tewdwr – at Leeds. Their grandson became Henry VII, who founded the Tudor dynasty.

The castle is open to the public at advertised times.

Oast Houses

In spring the Kentish Weald, with its red-brick oast houses, apple orchards and grazing sheep is one of the prettiest places in England. In the first century when the Romans entered Kent they found civilized farmers, unlike the rest of England which was inhabited by wandering tribes. The Romans planted cherry orchards and vines, and the Normans introduced pears. Hops came from the Continent in 1538 ('Hops, reformation, bayes and beer came to England all in a year'). Today's hop gardens cover 10,000 acres of Kent.

The nineteenth century oast houses with their conical red roofs and ventilating cowls have been superseded by less picturesque but more efficient drying sheds. The oast, or kiln, was an open fire burning on the floor of this brick building (usually circular to conserve heat). Smokeless fuel was burned, to preserve the flavour of the hops spread to dry on horse-hair netting and wood slats, about 12 feet above the fire. The hops were laid to cool in an adjacent building, then packed into canvas bags, or pokes, for the brewery. Now, as then, dried hops are added to bitter beer when it is 'wort' – malt, dried and ground, and boiled in water. There they stand for a day or so clarifying, preserving and flavouring, as the mixture cools.

Hops grow rapidly, up to an inch in 24 hours, starting from the ground around Mayday and climbing up strings to permanent wires 15 to 20 feet overhead by the third week in June. The elaborate art of hop-tying, performed by men on stilts, is one country skill that has not been bettered by modern technology.

From late August through September the ripened female catkins are picked, nowadays largely by machine, once by 'foreigners' from London's East End. Whole families worked arduously, camping in often insanitary conditions to earn their small wages. Some still come, although most hop picking is done by young students as a summer vacation job. Modern attitudes and bye-laws guarantee proper conditions but the comradely spirit, bred in harder times, still exists.

Polperro

Polperro was, until the mid-twentieth century, a typical Cornish fishing village. Now predominantly a tourist resort, its considerable charms are set out for visitors who must leave their cars in parking lots above, and scramble down the precipitous streets past colour-washed cottages and gift shops to the tiny harbour below. Between the streets, close to the backs of the houses, a stream called the Rafiel rushes down. On either side of the town the lofty cliffs rising from the sea are covered, in early summer, with ice plants.

The streets are interconnected by a network of alleys and the stream is crossed by stone bridges. The House on Props, a restaurant, juts over the water by the Roman Bridge. By the Saxon Bridge is the house, now a museum, where for 60 years the grandfather of the scholar and writer, Sir Arthur Quiller-Couch, lived and worked. Dr Jonathan Couch, an eminent naturalist and historian, was the village doctor and a much-loved character. His writing desk, manuscripts, drawings and all manner of curios are on view, as well as smuggling and fishing relics.

This coast, with its deep creeks, was ideal for smuggling and when duty was levied on tobacco in 1660, French, Flemish and Cornish ships began dealing in the contraband. Polperro grew to be such a flourishing centre that in the late nineteenth century the Preventive Measures were established. Many of the cottages still have their smuggling cellars, and there is a smuggling museum near the harbour, in Talland Road.

Among the working fishing boats are boats for hire, or in fine weather, for trips around the wooded hilly inlets of Cornwall's lovely east and south coasts.

Salisbury Cathedral

Salisbury Cathedral is one of the most beautiful and one of the most architecturally important of British cathedrals and its milky spire dominates the skyline of Salisbury Plain and of the valleys and meadow lands around. The city itself stands at the junction of three rivers, the Nadder, fed by the Wylye at Wilton, the Bourne and the Avon. Two miles north on the Plain the abandoned site of Old Sarum plaintively demonstrates the

POLPERRO
Overleaf: Set between high cliffs, this picturesque village, with its lime-washed houses, is one of the most charming in the West Country.

OAST HOUSE
Right: The conical roof of an oast house can be seen behind this Kent farmhouse. Oast houses were formerly used to dry hops, which are still one of the main products of this fertile county.

effect of geography upon history.

Roman Old Sarum became the Saxons' Searo-byrg, or 'dry town', and later was the site of a cathedral built by William I's nephew, Bishop Osmund. In 1220, Bishop Richard Poore found Old Sarum too dry and too exposed, so he laid out a new town to the south, on lush meadows, at the meeting of the rivers. Today Salisbury is a rich mix of medieval, Georgian and Victorian streets with some twentieth century shopping precincts, but still retaining Bishop Poore's grid plan, his medieval bridges and his Cathedral. This early English Gothic structure is unaltered, but for the elegant additions of cloisters and chapter house in the late thirteenth century, and in 1334 the spire. It is over 400 feet high, and still the tallest in England. In the Cathedral library is Christopher Wren's report of 1668 on the spire, which turned out to be too heavy for its supports which which were put out of alignment, but the Cathedral, Wren said, 'may be justly accounted one of the finest patterns of the architecture of the age wherein it was built'.

The Cathedral remains unaltered but much has been taken away, particularly at the end of the eighteenth century when the Close was levelled and the graves removed. But with its beautiful medieval houses, the Close, still entered through fourteenth century gates, is one of the finest and most serene of its kind. At this time, too, the architect James Wyatt deprived the nave of screens, tombs, stained glass and other treasures. Much, however, remains. Columns of Purbeck marble, and the beautifully restored octagonal Chapter House, fan vaulted, embellished with sculptures and ancient stained glass; the library with one of the four original copies of the Magna Carta, and with writings by Geoffrey de Monmouth and Bede; all, and much else, gathered under one

SALISBURY CATHEDRAL
Left: Built mainly between 1220 and 1284, this is one of the most architecturally unified of English cathedrals.

original design.

The man responsible for that design, Bishop Poore, laid the first foundation stone for the Pope, the second for the Archbishop of Canterbury, and the third for himself. In Salisbury's great surrounding wall and in its tower are stones from Richard Poore's first Bishopric – the Cathedral at Old Sarum.

Stonehenge

Stonehenge is one of the finest prehistoric sites in Europe. Its purpose is not yet understood, although authorities believe that it had a religious significance associated with sun worship. Neolithic tribes made the outer circle of ditch and bank, enclosing another circle of 56 pits, some used for burials, all ritually refilled. Two or three thousand years later between 1700 and 1600 B.C., Beaker People (so called from pots found among their remains) brought blue stones by sea and river from Pembroke's Prescelly Hills, some 200 miles from Salisbury Plain in Wiltshire where the great circle stands. Setting up the stones within the Neolithic works they contrived the stone

circle, an avenue and the Neolithic Heel or Sun stone, standing in the centre of the outer circle, to align at the rising of the midsummer sun.

Powerful Bronze Age traders altered the circle by removing the blue stones and setting up huge Sarsen ones of sandstone, which they brought from the Marlborough Downs, close to Avebury, where there is a far larger but not so dramatically situated circle. These stones were 'dressed' so as to accommodate the lintels set across two uprights (trilithons). Later in the Bronze Age, in two separate phases, the Beaker People's blue stones were set up in horseshoe and oval shapes and this, largely, is what remains. Ancient alignments were honoured, and on June 21st the sun can be seen from the so-called 'Altar' stone at the heart of the Henge, rising over the Heel stone.

Stonehenge's creation spanned 900 years. It has always been a sacred and mysterious place, and to this day the Companions of the Most Ancient Order of Druids gather at midnight so that they might observe the midsummer sunrise on June 21st.

Shakespeare's Birthplace and Anne Hathaway's Cottage

Stratford-upon-Avon, where Shakespeare was born and died, is visited by about a million people a year, drawn by sights such as Anne Hathaway's cottage and other places associated with England's greatest poet. Yet Stratford-upon-Avon retains the character of a provincial market town with many of the houses, streets, markets and customs of Shakespeare's time. Not far from the market place (which holds a cattle market on Tuesdays and sells produce three days a week) is Henley Street, and the sixteenth century house where it is thought Shakespeare was born on 23 April 1564. Gabled and timber-framed, the interior is furnished as it would have been when Shakespeare's father, a glove maker and Alderman, ran a workshop in the east end of the house. This was a separate house used for business, and has been made a museum where one can see letters and documents such as the purchase deed of New House, then one of the finest houses in Stratford, bought by Shakespeare in 1597 after he had achieved success in London and at Queen Elizabeth's court. On the west side of the birthplace, which was the family dwelling, a room upstairs is presented as the bedroom where Shakespeare was born. Scratched on the window panes are the signatures of illustrious people like Ellen Terry, Henry Irving and Tennyson. Outside, the garden is planted with the bushes, herbs and flowers mentioned in Shakespeare's plays.

Even at the height of the season, visitors can follow the broad streets or narrow lanes from the birthplace to the schoolhouse, to Trinity Church which contains Shakespeare's tomb and memorial, to New House or to the beautiful Clopton Bridge (now sadly traffic bound) where Shakespeare walked as a boy.

Footpaths from Stratford still lead two miles west through fields to Shottery and Anne Hathaway's Cottage. This is, in fact, a fine fifteenth century yeoman's house by a brook, with a traditional English garden. Traditionally thought of as Anne Hathaway's birthplace (Shakespeare's bride was eight years his senior), the house has been the property of the Birthplace Trust since 1892. It suffered a fire in 1969 but was quickly restored, and visitors can see in its 12 rooms the appurtenances of sixteenth century domestic life. The kitchen has an open hearth with a clay oven, and in the parlour is the hard pillow settle on which no doubt Shakespeare sat many times. Beyond, the Forest of Arden once stretched. In these woods *As You Like It* was set. The surrounding Warwickshire countryside, reflected so many times in Shakespeare's plays, is relatively unchanged.

King Arthur's Castle, Tintagel

The ruins of a castle stand high above a shoreline of shingle and slate beaten by the Atlantic. Half is on the mainland, but the inner ward lies on an outcrop of rock linked by a fearful narrow path. This site is inextricably linked with Arthurian legend. Around A.D. 480 Igerna, wife of the Duke of Cornwall, was seduced by the King of the Britons, Uther Pendragon, who, with the help of Merlin the Magician, had taken on the image of Igerna's husband. Arthur, born at a castle which is said to have existed here, later became ruler of the Britons. A path leading down from the castle arrives at an opening in the cliff face which is still known as Merlin's Cave.

Another castle, built over the site of a Celtic monastery, was begun in 1145 by Reginald, Earl of Cornwall. One of its overlords was Edward, the Black Prince, the son of Edward III. Its structure was altered over the centuries, but by Elizabethan times it was in ruins. Beyond the castle remains are vestiges of the Celtic stone buildings that stood here from the sixth to the ninth century. The monks' dwellings face across the sea to Ireland and Wales.

The monks must have known, as the North Cornish do, the calm, sunny days of this otherwise treacherous coast ('From Padstow Point to Hartland Light is a watery grave by day or night'). It is a coast of mighty waves and tearing winds. On other days one is deprived of sight and sound by motionless thick mists, but in fine weather all is clear and an intense stillness pervades the island.

Windsor Castle

From the peaceful reaches of the Thames can be seen Windsor Castle, one of the Queen's residences and the largest inhabited castle in the world. The famous skyline, the work of Sir Jeffrey Wyatville for George IV, surmounts the town and trees. London is one hour's drive from Windsor.

47

William the Conqueror began the castle at the same time as he began the Tower of London, in 1078. He built near what was then an extensive forest close to Old Windsor, then known as Wyndsore. Since then the castle has been so changed that none of the Norman work remains. Almost every English sovereign since Edward III's reign has lived there, and almost every sovereign has made some alteration to its structure.

The castle has three parts. The Lower Ward includes St George's Chapel, said to be the most perfect example of English Perpendicular architecture, where six kings are buried. Hanging about the carved oak stalls are the banners and helmets of the Knights of the Garter, the order of chivalry founded by Edward III after a garter had been used by the King at the Battle of Crécy as a signal to attack. A ceiling of decorated fifteenth century fan vaulting covers the relics and tombs.

Henry II's Round Tower, built over the Norman castle, juts out from the Middle Ward, and from the top it is possible to look out across 12 counties. The State Apartments, which contain a priceless collection of paintings, furniture and armour, and the Queen's private apartments are in the Upper Ward. Here, too, Queen Mary's doll's house is displayed. Designed by Sir Edwin Lutyens as a replica of an early twentieth century grand residence, the doll's house is filled with paintings and furnishings in exquisite miniature. Even the tiny library contains books which were mostly written especially for the house.

The town of Windsor stands on a hill surrounded by river and parks. Home Park, on the river bank and close to the castle, is the burial place of Queen Victoria. The Great Park is open to the public, who come to walk or ride, or to see the heronry. Fallow deer graze among trees which in some parts of the park are 1000 years old. On the north bank of Virginia Water, the Valley Gardens are planted with the world's largest collection of rhododendron.

York Minster

York Minster, the largest Gothic cathedral in England and built over a period of two and a half centuries, combines the best Early English and Perpendicular styles of medieval architecture. But the ultimate glory is in the Minster's magnificent medieval stained glass.

The present cathedral was begun in 1220 by Archbishop Walter de Grey, and finished in 1480. The luminous quality of the limestone belies the great mass of the cathedral with its vast battlemented lantern tower, wide Early English transepts and two noble towers in the Perpendicular style at the western end. Since the completion of the towers the cathedral has remained structurally unaltered, although parts of the interior have twice been restored as a result of fire, and today a massive rescue operation is in hand to strengthen the foundations. In 1644, Sir Thomas Fairfax, after the battle of Marston Moor, gave orders to the victorious Parliamentarians to spare the Minster, and in World War II the windows were removed. Cleaning, releading, repiercing and replacing are still in progress.

The cathedral is approached from Stonegate, one of medieval York's best preserved streets, and can be entered under the magnificent Rose window by the south door. The tall arches and columns, the vast spaciousness of the nave, the mass of carving and brasses, are illuminated by windows of glowing coloured glass. At the crossing of the transepts and the nave, four massive pillars and arches support the Lantern tower. The double aisles of the nave, with clustered columns supporting richly decorated arches, continue through the entrance of William Hindley's Perpendicular stone screen to the Choir with its great East Window, completed by John Thornton of Coventry in 1408. In the window are scenes from the Old Testament and the Book of Revelation across an area of 2000 square feet, the largest expanse of medieval stained glass in England.

York was an important centre for stained glass in the Middle Ages, and some of York Minster's windows come from the workshops of twelfth century Stonegate. The tradition is carried back to A.D. 699, when records first show the use of glass in an English church. Archbishop Wilfred used it in repairing a cathedral established on the site in 655 by King Oswald's brother, Oswy. He built over the ruins of a church where, in 627, Edwin, first Christian King of Northumbria, had been baptized.

York is one of the most attractive and prosperous of British cities and particularly rich in archaeological and architectural treasures, as well as first class museums. The Romans established a fort here, the Danes a colony and the Normans built defences on the foundations of the Roman wall. These medieval

fortifications remain relatively intact and visitors can walk around a three mile rampart to view the old city which, by the fourteenth century, was a major wool centre. There are many Tudor half-timbered houses to be seen along with fine Georgian dwellings built in the eighteenth century after the disasters of the Civil War. With the opening up of the railways in the nineteenth century York again became a major trading centre. Visitors should make an effort to see the splendid National Railway Museum, a delight for railway enthusiasts and non-specialists alike. The Castle Museum is one of Britain's leading museums with reconstructed streets and interiors from Tudor to Victorian times. Also worth a visit is the Yorkshire Museum, which houses extensive archaeological material from Roman York. The City of York Art Gallery houses a collection of European works.

The Brecon Beacons

The Brecons, wild mountains in a land of mountains, slope up from South Wales' mining valleys to the sandstone summits of Pen y Fan and Corn Ddu, Lofty Peak and Black Rock. The green peaks tower and overhang, rising sheer from the north. The vast glacial scoop between is Cadair Arthur, King Arthur's Chair. In clear weather from the highest peak, Pen y Fan, 2906 feet, one can see the Rhondda Valley and Ebbw Vale running to the Bristol Channel, with Somerset sometimes making a shadowy horizon. Facing north, the eye follows the Cambrian mountains, the backbone of Wales, towards Snowdonia. On rare days, the distant peak of Cader Idris appears. To the east of Brecon is Sugar Loaf, a once volcanic peak, which dominates the Usk as it thrusts between the Brecons and the Black Mountains

YORK MINSTER
The <u>West Front</u> *of York Minster dates from the first half of the fourteenth century, but this vast cathedral was begun 100 years earlier, and not completed until 1470. It contains some fine medieval stained glass. York fell in 867 to the Danes, who made it their capital and named it Jorvik, from which its present name is derived. Below: The* <u>East Front</u>, *sometimes compared to a sheer cliff face, contains a splendid window some seventy-eight feet high.*

June. 25, 1982

behind the market town of Abergavenny, the gateway to Brecon's National Park.

The Park's wild moors are roamed by ponies and grazed by sheep. A short distance from Abercrave the natural caverns, the Dan-yr-Ogof Caves, extend for over a mile. At the county town of Brecon the thirteenth century fortified Cathedral has a cresset stone, an ancient stone which held 30 cups for oil to light the Cathedral's lamps. Three and a half miles along the Merthyr Tydfil road, the Mountain Centre provides information about wildlife and Neolithic remains to be found in the Park. Brecon's Welsh name, Aberhonddu, echoes its position at the merging of the Honddu and the Usk, but the name 'Brecon' stems from the tribal name of earlier Irish invaders.

Just over two miles north-west of Brecon are the remains of a Roman fort. Early buildings were of timber and earth and second century stone remains have been found. The fort was occupied on and off until almost the end of the Roman occupation.

Caernarvon

Edward I built this impregnable castle in 1282 after defeating the Welsh princes, the Llewellyns. Dominating Wales' royal capital, Caernarvon, and the Menai Straits, the castle forms part of a line of coastal defences built along the north coast of Wales.

Edward's castles at Conway, Harlech and Caernarvon, known throughout Europe for their superior defences, incorporated ideas for fortification brought back from the Crusades. Caernarvon's triple turreted Eagle Tower, which with the Queen's tower was built over the Norman fortification, rises straight out of the water of the Menai Straits. The south face of the castle along the River Seiont allows for three tiers of archers, and parts of the castle have arrow slits designed for simultaneous use by three archers. The two Gatehouses, the King's and the Queen's, are equally forbidding.

The exterior is well preserved, but most of the interior has gone, the result of centuries of neglect. The castle was noted for the comparative comfort of its living quarters, perhaps as a result of Queen Eleanor's influence. Two years after the death of Llewellyn, 'the last true prince of Wales', and a year after Caernarvon was begun, the Queen gave birth to a son (1284). The infant prince, it was said, was presented to an unenthusiastic population as their future monarch, a prince born in Wales and 'a prince who could speak no English'.

CAERNARVON CASTLE
Caernarvon Castle's impregnability has been tested many times over the centuries. In 1403, when besieged by Owen Glendower and defended by only 28 men, its seven-to-eight-foot-thick walls withstood relentless bombardment by sophisticated siege machinery. During England's Civil War the castle changed hands several times but was finally taken by the Roundheads in 1646. Today Caernarvon is a popular tourist centre with facilities for boating, bathing and other sports. The town is especially lively on Saturday, which is Market Day.

Since then the castle has rarely been occupied or even visited by royal princes. By the sixteenth century it was in a ruined state and narrowly escaped destruction in the seventeenth century on order from Charles II. It was only at the beginning of this century that restoration began on the castle. The late Duke of Windsor (Prince Edward) was invested at Caernarvon in 1911, and the present Prince of Wales in 1969.

Portmeirion

Portmeirion in Merionethshire is Clough Williams-Ellis' creation of a Mediterranean fishing village on a spit of land between the Rivers Glaslyn and Dwyryd, where the Lleyn Peninsula meets the mainland. Started in 1926, this is a beauty spot without bungalows or souvenir shops. The architect Clough Williams-Ellis added to the indigenous plants and trees eucalyptus, cypresses and palms, and he created wild gardens of exotic plants. Now in this lush setting are houses and cottages, a restaurant, a hotel, a church and a lighthouse. Most buildings are in Italianate styles, but not rigidly so. The eighteenth century Bath House Colonnade was brought from Bristol in 1957 to save it from demolition, and a half-Romanesque, half-Baroque campanile (bell tower) echoes the white Mediterranean façades, columns, and classic statuary. The fine Portmeirion

Hotel was rebuilt by Williams-Ellis at the beginning of the scheme.

Around this peaceful and beautiful place, with the site of Gruffydd ap Cynan's twelfth century castle in the woods above, lie Caernarvonshire's slate quarried hills to the north. To the south is the dramatically sited Harlech Castle, with flats and estuaries between. At Borth-y-Gest, a bathing and boating village five miles west, visitors can play golf. In Portmeirion itself are fishing, swimming, tennis and walking facilities, and on the hillside behind the village are flower gardens. Long-term visitors can rent cottages. Day visitors are requested to pay a small entrance fee.

Snowdonia

The peaks of Snowdon are the highest in England and Wales, and the most awe-inspiring Yr Wyddfa, the summit at 3,560 feet, is the highest of Snowdon's five peaks whose razor-edged ridges stretch out like fingers across north-west Wales. The view from the top is of rock on rock, peak on peak, and glinting llyns, or lakes, cradled in the slate. Looking north-east, turning east and then south, one sees Elidir Fawr, Tryfan, the Glyder peaks, Carneddau, then Moel Siabod, with the Vale of Gwynant a slither of green backed by the distant Verwyn Mountains to the south-east. South across Ffestiniog are the Aran peaks and, at last, to the right of the mountain Rhinog Fawr is the glint of the sea. Harlech Castle, some 15 miles distant, guards the coast of Cardigan Bay. Turning full circle, one sees the wind-swept Lleyn Peninsula thrusting between Cardigan and Caernarvon Bays.

Snowdonia National Park extends south and south-east to take in Lake Bala, Cader Idris and Aberdovey, which introduce softer aspects. Flanking Snowdonia proper is the Conway Vale with the woodland beauty of Betws-y-Coed, Fairy Glen and the Swallow Falls. But the Park protects the isolated grandeur of a land where man's only mark has been the gouging of slate quarries into the valleys. This wilderness, known as the Land of Eagles, is the habitat of a rare bird, the chough. Pine martens, red squirrels and polecats inhabit the slopes where trees grow. Otters catch salmon in the rivers, brown trout swim in the lakes, and in Lake Bala a white salmon, the gwyniad, is found. Like the fragile Mountain Spiderwort which grows in these parts, it is found nowhere else.

The Welsh have a special affection for Snowdonia. In the thirteenth century the mountains were a natural stronghold of the Llewellyns against King Edward I. After his defeat Llewellyn ap Gryffydd followed his youngest brother, Dafydd, to Dolbadarn, a tower high over a valley at the lower end of Llyn Peris. Dafydd's other brother, Owain, was held for 20 years in this tower after attempting to take over Llewellyn's share in their joint rule over Wales.

But Snowdonia is a region of climbers and hikers. There are several routes to the summit, varying from sedentary (by steam train from Llanberis) to 'very difficult', in climbing terms. One of the most celebrated ascents is in September by the light of a harvest moon.

Tenby

Tenby is one of the finest examples intact of a British medieval walled town. The old houses, narrow streets and thirteenth century walls stand on limestone cliffs thrusting into the sea, with wide sands north and south.

Tenby began as a fishing station for Danes coming south via Scotland in pre-Norman times, and in the twelfth century it was settled by Flemish weavers. Welsh raids prompted the construction of the walls. There is a well preserved merchant's house, recently restored by the National Trust, which reports in its Guide that 'when the building was restored the late medieval painted floral decoration in red, black and yellow, on the only original interior partition that survives, emerged from beneath no fewer than 23 coats of whitewash'. The Trust also protects the early fifteenth century Plantagenet house next door. Castle Hill, on the tip of Tenby's promontory, has a local museum with prehistoric remains, a fine art collection and exhibits from Caldy Island, just over two miles south. This splendid resort has cliff-top hotels, facilities for tennis and bowls, a golf course and a yacht club.

Motor launches make trips to Caldy Island with its beautiful coastline, lighthouse and colonies of sea birds and seals. An ancient priory church, a rare Celtic ogham stone with an indecipherable Gaelic script whose inventor, in the fourth century A.D., was probably familiar with the Roman alphabet, are of historical interest. The modern Cistercian Abbey permits male visitors at prescribed hours. The monks make perfume from the flowers on the island which is sold in Tenby.

SNOWDONIA
Overleaf: Snowdonia is the highest mountain range in England and Wales, though its peaks are no more than the worn-down stubs of vast, ancient rock fields thrust up by the earth's movement 300 million years ago.

TENBY
Right: In medieval times this was the principal fortified town of South Wales; during the reign of Elizabeth I it was further strengthened against the threat of the Spanish Armada. Its medieval walls were surmounted by perhaps as many as 20 towers, which were probably constructed by order of William de Valence, Earl of Pembroke.

London

One of London's most potent symbols—Tower Bridge. It is the most easterly of the capital's 23 road bridges over the Thames.

The British Museum in Bloomsbury

The British Museum is one of the world's largest and greatest treasure houses. Its famous collection of antiquities includes exhibits from Egyptian, Assyrian, Greek and Roman, British, Oriental and Asian cultures. It houses, in addition, a vast number of priceless books and manuscripts. The domed Reading Room (used by scholars but not open to the public) and the collections are housed in an early-Victorian classic building on the site of Montague House, which had been bought by public lottery in 1753 to accommodate the natural history collection of the physician Sir Hans Sloane, and the Cotton and Harley collections of manuscripts. By 1759, when the museum opened, the collections were expanding rapidly through government purchases, gifts and bequests. The expansion continues today. Collections and displays are subject to constant revision, so that even regular visitors cannot claim to have seen all there is.

The visiting sightseer can explore at will or join lecture tours on weekdays (excluding Mondays). Generally accepted as priority exhibits are the treasures from the ancient Assyrian and Greek and Roman civilizations in the west wing. Along the outer flank of this wing in the specially-built Duveen Gallery are the famous Elgin Marbles from Athens' Parthenon. An extensive, graceful frieze is displayed all around the gallery, along with sculptures depicting the battle between the Lapiths and the Centaurs, the contest between Athena and Poseidon, and the birth of Athens.

Even if no more than a superficial visit can be made, the visitor should not miss the Egyptian mummies and the famous Rosetta Stone, which provided the key to the deciphering of ancient Egyptian hieroglyphics. Also to be seen are the colossal Assyrian lions and winged bulls, and the Sumerian and Babylonian artifacts.

In the Manuscript Saloon on the south-east corner of the ground floor, the visitor can see the delicate *Lindisfarne Gospels*, illuminated by the Saxon Bishop Eadfrith around A.D. 700, and the Venerable Bede's *Ecclesiastical History of the English People* dating back to the eighth century. Other important, and later, displays in this gallery include two of the original four copies of the Magna Carta; a Deed of Mortgage signed by William Shakespeare; and two of Nelson's log books from HMS *Victory*.

Outside the museum in Great Russell Street and Museum Street are the Theosophy bookshop, a Scottish knitwear shop, Collet's Chinese Gallery and Davenports' joke shop, popular with children, but also patronized by professional magicians. Museum Street leads into Bloomsbury Way where, in sight of Bloomsbury Square, is the Corinthian portico of Nicholas Hawksmoor's Church of St George's, built in 1716, its steeple surmounted by a statue of George I.

Bloomsbury Square, the first in the Bloomsbury development, was laid out in 1665. It is linked by Bedford Row to Russell Square, lying north. Twentieth-century blocks have altered the harmony of the development (largely carried out by the land-owning family of the Dukes of Bedford after 1800), but some examples remain complete, notably Bedford Square, with its original town houses, and the beautiful Woburn Walk in the north-east of Bloomsbury. This is a sheltered pedestrian terrace of elegant, well-preserved shop fronts. Dickens lived and worked close by in Tavistock Square which, with Gordon Square, is associated with the writers and artists including Virginia Woolf, Lytton Strachey, Clive Bell, remembered as the Bloomsbury Group. The Courtauld Institute in Woburn Square contains, among other interesting works, the finest collection of French Impressionist painting to be found in Britain.

There are other museums that should not be missed if one has the opportunity. The National Gallery, in Trafalgar Square, is one of the greatest art museums in the world with a collection that represents some of the finest European painting from the thirteenth to the early twentieth century. It is particularly rich in Dutch, Flemish and Italian Masters.

The Tate Gallery, along the Embankment, houses three distinct collections: British painting from the sixteenth century to the present day; modern foreign painting from the French Impressionists onwards; and modern sculpture. The Tate continues to add to its collection through purchases of contemporary work.

Buckingham Palace

The most famous of the Queen's residences, Buckingham Palace stands in 40 acres of garden at the corner of two of London's most charming parks, St James's Park and Green Park. Constitu-

tion Hill leads between the secluded palace gardens and the grassy unfenced terrain of Green Park to Hyde Park Corner. The classic-style east façade, fronted by a gravelled forecourt and sturdy black iron railings, is the best known view of Buckingham Palace. This is where sightseers gather to catch a glimpse of the Royal family or to watch the Changing of the Guard at 11.30 a.m. The Royal Standard, when flying from the masthead, proclaims that the Queen is in residence.

Buckingham House was built for the Duke of Buckingham in 1703. George III bought it, and Nash improved it for William IV between 1824 and 1836. Queen Victoria conferred the title 'palace' when she moved here on her accession in 1837.

The east wing was added in 1847, and Nash's Marble Arch, which stood facing the original three wings was removed to the top of Park Lane, where it is today. In 1912 Sir Aston Webb remodelled the east front during three months while King George V and Queen Mary were out of town. The builders were invited to dinner at the palace as a reward for their quick work.

George VI moved to Buckingham Palace in 1937 and, together with his Queen, remained through World War II. Prince Charles was born here in 1948; Queen Elizabeth moved to the palace after her accession. At royal births, marriages and accessions, and in time of grave national crisis, crowds keep vigil outside the black iron railings.

This part of the palace faces directly

CAMDEN LOCK
Slightly off the well-trodden tourist path, Camden Lock is a lively corner of London where skilled craftsmen work and sell their wares. It is also the embarkation point for a cruise by barge along the Regent's Canal.

down the broad, proud Mall to Admiralty Arch. In the centre of the pink tarmac space outside the palace railings Sir Aston Webb's elaborate monument to Queen Victoria, surmounted by her statue in white marble, gazes down the Mall along the route of royal processions bound for Trafalgar Square, Whitehall and thence to Westminster.

The Mall, fringed by St James's Park to the south, was broadened and double-lined with plane trees as part of the memorial to Queen Victoria in 1911. At the approach to Admiralty Arch is Nash's Carlton House Terrace, facing the park across the Mall. These massive aristocratic mansions were built between 1827 and 1832, and are approached by the Duke of York Steps. The Grand Old Duke (who had 10,000 men in the nursery rhyme and was Commander in Chief of the Army from 1795 to 1827) is commemorated by a bronze statue, a column of Tuscan granite 124 feet high, erected in 1834 and paid for by stopping army pay for one day. Carlton House Terrace is occupied by such varied organizations as the Royal Society at No 6, the Commonwealth Secretariat at No 10, and Crockford's, London's most famous gaming club, at No 16.

The public is not admitted to the palace or its surroundings, unless invited to attend royal functions like the famous garden parties. In Buckingham Gate, however, is the Royal Mews, and here visitors can see the Queen's horses and carriages, landaus and coaches. Specially trained staff take care of the horses, the elaborately adorned State Coach used for coronations, the Glass Coach used by royal brides, the Irish State Coach in which the Queen is driven to the opening of Parliament, and any other royal conveyances. Also open to the public in Buckingham Gate, the Queen's Gallery shows pictures from the large and varied royal collections. Once the private chapel of Buckingham Palace, it was bombed during the Second World War, and has been rebuilt since then as part private chapel, part art gallery.

Camden Lock and Little Venice on Regent's Canal

The woodyard and wharves of Camden Lock on the Regent's Canal, closed because of twentieth century financial pressures, were commercially redeveloped by a group of artists and craft workers in the late 1960s. They renovated many of the handsome eighteenth century warehouses and established a flourishing market and crafts centre in the midst of the traditional working-class area of Camden Town. The market, operating at weekends, offers finely-made jewellery, fashions, trimmings and household accessories, as well as antiques and second-hand goods.

On weekdays, open workshops operate in canal buildings around a cobbled courtyard adjacent to the market. Here under such names as Blind Alley (individually designed roller blinds), Lead and Light (stained glass to order), The Five Jewellers and The Three Potters, craft specialists carry out traditional skills and explore new methods for producing useful, unusual and well-designed wares. Here also are friendly restaurants, including one on a floating barge, which offer a wide range of cuisine and a variety of stalls selling appealing and unusual refreshments. A popular attraction for young people is Dingwalls, a well-established disco and club which has a friendly atmosphere, particularly during the week, and where up-and-coming folk, rock, and jazz musicians play. The future of Camden Lock is, however, uncertain. This spontaneous development is on a site wanted for offices and shops. The commercial pressures that closed the canals continue to threaten the craft workers and the market.

Camden Lock is the embarkation point for the *Jenny Wren*, an original narrow boat (as some barges were called) which offers trips along the Regent's Canal. Passing the Park and the Zoo, it links the bustle of Camden Lock with a residential enclave of Victorian and twentieth century canalside dwellings, known as Little Venice.

Little Venice is centred on the triangular Paddington basin at the starting point of the Regent's Canal. The basin shelters houseboats, small private launches and an art gallery. Canoes can be hired and visitors can row to the tiny island of weeping willows, called Browning's Island after the poet, who lived nearby. The precincts of the basin are open to the public during the daytime, and the tow path affords a peaceful walk as far as Camden Lock. In the summer the British Waterways Board's water-buses operate from here, leaving every hour on the hour for the Zoo, and a narrow boat, *Jason's Trip*, operates excursions to Camden Lock.

Each point of the canal basin's triangle

receives a branch of the canal. The most tranquil and the loveliest part of Little Venice is to be found along the northeast arm of the canal as it runs between Blomfield Road and Maida Avenue, overlooked by sheltered Victorian semi-detached villas set in luxuriant gardens. As the two streets, one on either side of the canal, rise to meet the Edgware Road at the far end, the canal disappears into a tunnel on its way to Regent's Park and Camden Lock. There are pleasant pubs in the area, some overlooking the canal.

Chelsea

Chelsea Embankment and Cheyne Walk, with other peaceful residential backwaters beyond the river, make Chelsea a delightful place to visit. Once a riverside village, and in the nineteenth century the rendezvous of 'bohemian' artists and writers, Chelsea became the trend-setter of the Swinging Sixties. It is still, perhaps, the mecca for young people but there persists in Chelsea the comfortable atmosphere of a friendly village. The King's Road, running between Fulham Road and the Thames, is a lively shopping centre with undistinguished architecture – although Chelsea Town Hall makes an imposing Victorian interruption among the 1960s coffee bars and boutiques – that leads south-west from Sloane Square past the World's End junk shops into Fulham. Towards the Fulham end, the King's Road's bistros, exotic boutiques, launderettes and Chinese take-aways become interspersed with high class antique shops, rare book shops, watchmakers' and other small specialist establishments.

Between Fulham Road to the north and the King's Road are quiet comfortable residences. Georgian terraces like Old Church Street are lined with tall, narrow, well-cared-for town houses. But it is the region between the King's Road and the river that provides historical associations of interest to the visitor.

Old Church Street crosses the King's Road and meets the river at Cheyne Walk, a well-known stretch of early nineteenth century houses, some with balconies and delicate ironwork, fronting narrow public gardens along Chelsea Embankment. At the western end, at No 118 Cheyne Walk, the painter Turner spent his last years. Many other eminent artists and writers of the late nineteenth and early twentieth centuries lived around Cheyne Walk, and there are a

number of commemorative blue plaques. Whistler lived at No 96, where he painted the essayist and historian Thomas Carlyle, the 'sage of Chelsea', who lived for 46 years in the quiet side road, Cheyne Row. The Queen Anne house, now No 24, belongs to the National Trust and may be visited. A ring at the bell gains admittance, and the courteous attention of the guide. The visitors' book is signed with a quill pen. The interior is dark, discreet and simply furnished. There are many mementos and in Carlyle's top-floor study (which he built in a vain attempt to avoid noisy neighbours) are fascinating nineteenth century photographs, one showing Carlyle in his garden, straw-hatted and smoking a pipe.

Rossetti, Meredith and Swinburne lived for a time at No 16 Cheyne Walk, and George Eliot died at No 4. Both Oscar Wilde and Augustus John lived at one time in Tite Street. Chelsea Old Church, which dates from the twelfth century, contains a huge number of sixteenth and seventeenth century monuments, including a memorial to Sir Thomas More, one of Chelsea's most famous residents. On the north side is a graceful reclining monument, attributed to Bernini, to Lady Jane Cheyne, wife of the lord of the manor who died in 1669. Among other interesting items are the chained books, the only ones in any London church, given by physician and naturalist Sir Hans Sloane who died in 1753, and whose tomb is in the churchyard.

Chelsea's river front, the Embankment, stretches east from Battersea Bridge to the graceful Chelsea Bridge which has a fine view of Battersea Power Station. In between is Albert Bridge, a combined cantilever and suspension bridge. The Embankment at this eastern end runs alongside Chelsea Hospital, founded in Charles II's reign as a home for veteran soldiers. Wren's fine brick building with colonnade and cupola is seen across an expanse of public gardens which extend to Chelsea Bridge Road, and then north, as Ranelagh Gardens, to Lower Sloane Street. At this end the gardens are a pleasant wilderness of paths, trees and flowering shrubs. The Chelsea Pensioners, scarlet-coated in summer and dark-coated in winter, are a familiar sight along the Chelsea streets. On application, one of the Pensioners will show visitors the hospital and grounds.

Chelsea's summer event, the magnificent Chelsea Flower Show, is held in the

CHEYNE WALK
Overleaf: One of the most elegant streets in Chelsea, Cheyne Walk overlooks the Thames. Among its gracious eighteenth century houses is the home of Thomas Carlyle, which is open to the public.

THE CHELSEA FLOWER SHOW
Right: A highlight of the London year, the Chelsea Flower Show takes place in May in the grounds of the Royal Hospital. Masses of prize blooms, plants and trees and landscaped gardens, complete with ponds and ornamental bridges, make the Flower Show a source of inspiration for gardeners and a visual delight for everyone.

spacious Hospital Gardens. Whole gardens are laid out for display, and first class exhibits include all the principal flowering plants.

Fleet Street

Fleet Street, the centre of England's national newspaper industry, runs west from Temple Bar (where the Queen, if she wishes to enter the City, must ceremoniously obtain permission from the Lord Mayor) to Ludgate Circus. The newspaper offices are centred around this, the City end of Fleet Street, where St Paul's can be seen on distant Ludgate Hill. The *Daily Telegraph* and the *Daily Express* buildings dominate the north side, the first a huge, somewhat ornate 1930s building, the latter built in 1931, with rounded corners, black glass and chrome. Opposite along Whitefriars Street and Bouverie Street are sited the *News of the World* (Whitefriars), the *Daily Mail* and the magazine *Punch*. East on this side at No 85 is the office housing Reuter's and the Press Association; opposite is the evening paper, *The New Standard*, in Shoe Lane. Periodicals and provincial newspapers are printed in Fleet Street, and the other national dailies are within walking (or running) distance. The newspaper houses will arrange tours if they receive notice but Fleet Street is perhaps best seen after 10 p.m. when the huge newsprint lorries and the brightly-lit offices and busy cafes convey a sense of urgency and industry.

In the daytime, one can see much of old London in the maze of Courts and Lanes behind Fleet Street. Past the *Daily Telegraph* building is Wine Office Court, and the charming tavern, Ye Olde Cheshire Cheese, still with wooden benches and sanded floor. Farther along is Dr Johnson's seventeenth century house, at No 17 Gough Square, where he lived from 1749 to 1758. Among other memorabilia are prints of Dr Johnson and his associates Burke, Boswell and Goldsmith. Upstairs in the attic Johnson wrote his Dictionary.

Around here are Fleet Street's taverns and coffee houses – Peele's at the corner of Fetter Lane, the Clachan in Mitre Court, the Rainbow, El Vino and the famous Cock Tavern. Near Middle Temple Lane at No 17 Fleet Street is the house of Prince Henry, James I's son who died prematurely before he could take the throne. At No 1 Fleet Street is Child's Bank, founded 1671, and whose customers included Oliver Cromwell,

Samuel Pepys and Nell Gwynn. It is now housed in a nineteenth century building.

Between Chancery Lane and Fetter Lane is the last church of the City, St Dunstan's in-the-West, rebuilt in Gothic style in 1829, but with its original clock of 1671 on which two giants strike the hour. Here the poet John Donne was vicar from 1624 to 1631, with Izaac Walton (whose *Compleat Angler* was published from offices in the nearby St Dunstan's Churchyard) as vestryman from 1629 to 1644. Beyond Temple Bar at Aldwych is St Clements Dane, famed in the nursery rhyme for its bells.

Back at the heart of Fleet Street behind Reuter's in St Bride's Lane, is St Bride's Church, built between 1701 and 1703 by Wren. It has his tallest, and perhaps loveliest, five-tiered spire. Pepys was baptized in the old church in 1633. There is a museum in the crypt. This, 'The Cathedral of Fleet Street', was badly damaged by bombs in the 1940s but restored with funds from the newspaper industry in 1957. During the rebuilding a cache of Roman remains, and a number of seventeenth and eighteenth century skeletons, were found.

Greenwich

Greenwich is one of the prettiest and most important of London's villages. Its waterfront architecture, the Royal Naval College and the National Maritime Museum overlooked by the Royal Observatory from the hill, gives Greenwich a river approach of unrivalled splendour. Its Royal history reaches back to the fifteenth century when one of London's greatest palaces was built here by Humphrey, Duke of Gloucester. Henry VIII and his daughters Mary and Elizabeth were born in this palace which occupied the site where the Royal Naval College now stands.

Close to Greenwich Pier, in dry dock, are the *Cutty Sark* and *Gypsy Moth IV*, the former the most famous of the nineteenth century tea-clippers, the latter the twentieth century ketch in which Sir Francis Chichester sailed single-handed around the world in 1966–1967. Both ships are open to visitors all the year round. The *Cutty Sark*, 280 feet long, was built at Dumbarton in 1869. Her figurehead represents the witch Nannie, featured in Robert Burns' poem *Tam O'Shanter*, who wore a short shift, or 'cutty sark'. Many maritime relics are displayed on board and the size of the crew's living quarters give an idea of the sailors' grim working conditions. There

NATIONAL MARITIME MUSEUM, GREENWICH
Overleaf: The Museum houses exhibits illustrating Britain's maritime history, from Tudor times to World War II. Ship models, uniforms and navigation instruments are among the objects on display. In the distance is the Queen's House, designed by Inigo Jones for Queen Anne, wife of James I. Other attractions at Greenwich include the Old Royal Observatory and the Royal Hospital, both designed by Wren.

FLEET STREET
Right: This bustling street houses the majority of England's national newspaper offices. Behind its frenzy, however, the visitor can find a few oases of quiet, such as Dr. Johnson's House in Gough Square, and St. Bride's Church, with its tree-shaded courtyard.

HYDE PARK
*Right and Overleaf:
Formerly owned by the
Crown, Hyde Park was
given to the public by
Charles I in 1637. Together
with the adjoining
Kensington Gardens it
forms the largest park in
central London. Its main
feature is the Serpentine, an
artificial lake on which one
may go boating. Horseback
riding can be enjoyed on
Rotten Row—the old* Route
du Roi, *or 'King's Way'.
At the northeast corner of the
park orators of various
persuasions hold forth on
Sundays; at the southeast
corner is Apsley House, the
elegant home of the Duke of
Wellington, which is open to
the public.*

*GREENWICH
Left: One of the two domed
towers of Wren's Royal
Naval Hospital, now the
Royal Naval College, one
of Greenwich's several
attractions.*

is a magnificent exhibition of ships' figureheads in the lower hold.

The Royal Naval College is reached first. This building was begun in the mid-seventeenth century by Charles II on the site of the sixteenth century royal palace. Only part of the west wing was completed but building was resumed in the reign of William and Mary when Sir Christopher Wren was employed to design it as a hospital for retired seamen. The Hospital was opened in 1702 and remained in use until 1873. Under one of its twin domes is the Chapel and under the other the magnificent Painted Hall, built by Wren and with ceiling and wall paintings by James Thornhill.

The body of Lord Nelson lay in state in the Upper Hall and in the grounds of the Naval College, Sir Francis Chichester received his knighthood from Queen Elizabeth II in 1967. A pleasant walk along the pier arrives at the Trafalgar Tavern, a noted riverside inn. From there, the Queen's House can be reached by way of Park Row.

The Queen's House, centre of the National Maritime Museum, is the earliest example of Palladian architecture in England. It was designed for Anne of Denmark, James I's Consort, by Inigo Jones, and completed in 1635. It is linked by colonnades to early nineteenth century east and west wings. The museum houses a unique collection of artifacts, sea-going craft, maritime relics, uniforms, medals and fine paintings, and it is an international centre for historical maritime research. Exhibits date from Tudor times to the seventeenth century.

In rooms nine and ten, among portraits and autographs, the Nelson Collection shows the uniform worn by Nelson at the battle of Trafalgar, the

jacket torn by the bullet that killed him. Also displayed are his Bible, grog jug and purse. In the Navigation room is a fine collection of charts and nautical instruments; and the New Neptune Hall's displays of prehistoric wooden boats, coracles, modern vessels and royal barges (notably Queen Mary's shallop of 1689) must catch the imagination.

Behind the museum building Greenwich Park sweeps up to Flamstead House which accommodated the Royal Observatory from 1675 to 1940, when deteriorating atmospheric conditions forced its removal to Herstmonceux in Sussex. Historic astronomical equipment is displayed inside, and 1 p.m. is marked every day by the drop of a time ball, carried by a mast on the roof since 1833, which is visible to shipping on the Thames. On the terrace, visitors can stand a foot each side of a brass strip denoting the zero meridian.

Hyde Park and Kensington Gardens

Hyde Park and Kensington Gardens together form the largest park in central London. More than 600 acres of grass, trees, waters and ornamental gardens lie here at the heart of West London, contained between Knightsbridge and Bayswater Road, stretching from Park Lane on the east boundary to Kensington Palace on the west. Hyde Park and Kensington Gardens are officially divided by a fine arched stone bridge across the tree-fringed lake lying diagonally north-south, created in 1730 by Caroline of Anspach, the wife of George II. The Hyde Park side of the lake is called the Serpentine, and in Kensington Gardens, the Long Water.

Hyde Park was once part of the Manor of Hyde, and the property of Westminster Abbey. After the Dissolution of the Monasteries, Henry VIII took over the park for hunting. Charles I opened it to the public a century later, but in 1730 Kensington Gardens was appropriated as a private pleasure garden for Gecrge II's queen, under whose direction the broad avenues and well laid out gardens were planned. Today both parks form a huge, informal area where the public can ride, fish, swim, row, walk and fly kites.

The main areas of activity centre on the Serpentine. The rest of Hyde Park is a wide green space gently sloping north to Marble Arch. At the meeting of Park Lane and Marble Arch at Speakers' Corner popular orators can be heard at weekends expounding on all manner of diverse subjects.

Near Hyde Park Corner in the southeast the old Route du Roi, Rotten Row, leads west for a mile. This sandy track, once a fashionable parade for horse-drawn carriages, is still reserved for horses and riders. Between Rotten Row and Carriage Road, the Great Exhibition of 1851 was staged in Crystal Palace (later removed to Sydenham). On the other side of Rotten Row, at the south end, the tip of the Serpentine, the Dell, has a small arcadian garden and an open air summer-time café. Just across the water the bank is reserved for fishing. Five hundred permits are issued each season and bream, carp, dace and gudgeon are caught. Farther along on the south shore is the Lido, where there are bathing pavilions, and on the opposite shore boats can be hired. The Serpentine Art Gallery nearby holds summertime exhibitions. It faces the futuristically designed Serpentine Restaurant and ring road, which leads across the lake to the lush woods of Kensington Gardens.

The far end of the lake, due south of Lancaster Gate Underground, was once a duck pond. Now there are charming Italianate gardens, with sculptures and fountains. In this, the north part of Kensington Gardens, is a dogs' cemetery, a children's playground in the far north-west corner, and a small bird sanctuary. Over to the west the Broad Walk, a beautiful avenue of sycamore backed with limes, leads south past Kensington Palace and the Round Pond to the Flower Walk, and Kensington.

A great avenue of elms once led from the Round Pond which is directly east of the palace, past G. F. Watts' early twentieth century equestrian statue, Physical Energy, to the Long Water, and then beyond to Buck Hill in Hyde Park. From there, the magnificent view of the palace is known as the Vista. Since the disastrous Dutch Elm disease the double row of elms has been replaced with stripling oaks, sycamore and lime, and some of the avenue's majesty lost. Yet one can still gain some idea of how these planned walks looked when they were first planted for George I, early in the eighteenth century.

This part of the park, the wooded area between the palace and the Serpentine, is traditionally the beat of nannies and infants. A little way north, on the lakeside, is Sir George Frampton's statue of Peter Pan, a favourite with parents and children since its erection in 1912. The

Round Pond is popular with enthusiasts sailing model yachts. From there it is a short distance to the ornamental gardens of Kensington Palace, the only royal residence in London that opens its State Apartments to the public.

Art and Science in South Kensington

South Kensington is remarkable in that here, grouped together, are four of Britain's major museums. Between them they cover almost every aspect of science and the arts. They are popularly known as the Science Museum, the Geological Museum and the Natural History Museum. The Victoria and Albert Museum of Fine and Applied Arts is known as the V & A. The last two stand on opposite corners of Exhibition Road, near the pleasant centre of South Kensington.

On the west side is the Natural History Museum. An imposing structure of honey-coloured brick, liberally adorned with carved reptiles and plants, its interior is equally awe inspiring. The

interior has been redesigned recently and the layout of the exhibitions has changed quite dramatically. The main hall now contains a display of dinosaurs and other prehistoric reptiles together with a detailed learning programme on the relationships among reptiles. In addition, bays to the left and right of the large central gallery illustrate, in a series of clear, well-planned displays, the general principles of evolution. A similar series of displays on the development of man, formerly in this section, is now located upstairs in the museum.

Collections are arranged in scientific groupings (fish, mammals, plants and minerals) to provide equal interest for scientists and non-scientists. Of special interest to the visitor are the great dinosaur models, the life-size model of the 91 foot Blue Whale and the remarkable Bird Gallery. But these are the tip of the iceberg in a museum whose exhibits occupy three acres. Behind the scenes, five research departments employ about 300 scientists to make this a working museum. It is one of the principal international centres for classification and identification of plants, animals and minerals.

Across Exhibition Road is the equally impressive Victoria and Albert Museum in a vast white building with a colonnaded entrance approached by wide steps, surmounted by towers and an elaborate central dome.

The extensive collections of fine and applied arts covers all countries, styles and periods but with the greatest concentration of post-Classical European art and that of the Far East, India and Middle East. Within these broad groupings of time and place, called Primary Collections, are included the finest creations of decorative art. Among the exhibits in Room 52, which displays examples of Tudor art, are the Great Bed of Ware, 11 feet square and mentioned in Shakespeare's *Twelfth Night*, the Oxenburgh hangings worked by Mary Queen of Scots, and Elizabeth I's virginals. Next door are the incomparable Elizabethan miniatures by Isaac Oliver and Nicholas Hilliard, including the latter's *Young Man leaning against a tree among roses* and also two famous miniatures by Holbein. One floor down are displays of Sèvres china, and a work table that belonged to Queen Marie Antoinette in the eighteenth century.

In other parts of the building, Study Collections are grouped by class so that under the heading 'Ceramics', scholars may compare the development of tin-glazed earthenware in displays of Dutch Delft, French Faience and Italian Majolica (the best collection to be found outside Italy).

Among the collections of fine art are the world-famous Tapestry Cartoons of Raphael, which no visitor should miss, and a fine display of oil studies by John Constable.

The Science Museum, farther along Exhibition Road, in a series of demonstrations and displays, covers the history of science and its application to industry. The Entrance Hall has a Foucault Pendulum, which demonstrates the rotation of the earth on its axis. A display of beam engines, and demonstrations of animal, water and wind power beyond, introduce the museum's theme of the development of science and technology. Downstairs is an instructive children's section with models and dioramas, displays that can be 'worked', games, and a periscope through which one can see the Transport Gallery above. In the Transport Galleries visitors can see William Hedley's Puffing Billy of 1813, the world's oldest locomotive. Astronomical displays trace the science to early Egyptian times, and the aeronautical collection spans the years between Montgolfier's hot-air balloon, of which there is a model, and a range of aero-engines from steam-powered to jet.

A rotating globe in the entrance of the Geological Museum shows the geological make-up of the earth. In the centre of the hall, man's use of stones is illustrated by brilliant displays of cut and uncut gems, and decorative stones. Displays on either side show the geology of specific regions (for example, London and the Thames Valley), and deal with the effect of geological change on the life of man.

A modern addition to these classic displays illustrates, in a continuous projection on a screen, the origin of the earth, and the emergence of plant life. Volcanic action is shown in a film and in the Earthquake Room a recorded voice describes the development of an earthquake while the ground beneath the listeners' feet shakes in a convincing and frightening simulation of an actual seismic eruption.

Parliament Square and the Houses of Parliament

The wide thoroughfare of Whitehall leads south to Parliament Square where the great administrative centres of church and state, Westminster Abbey and the Houses of Parliament, are situated around an irregular area carpeted with grass, planted with gardens and adorned with statues of great statesmen. Bridge Street leads east over Westminster Bridge at Whitehall's approach to the square. On the corner of Bridge Street, Westminster Bridge and Parliament Square the Big Ben ('Big Ben' is actually the name of the bell, not the tower itself) clock tower appears to stand guard over the New Palace of Westminster.

That is the official title of the Houses of Parliament which occupy the site of Edward the Confessor's original palace on the riverside, and which form a dignified but sombre Victorian Gothic complex of turrets, pinnacles and spires, to the south-east of Parliament Square. The building was designed by Sir Charles Barry, who also laid out the square, after a fire had destroyed the remains of the palace in 1834. The elaborate Gothic detailing on the exterior of the building was nearly all produced by Augustus Pugin.

The House of Commons, located

HOUSES OF PARLIAMENT
Right: Built to a design by Sir Charles Barry, with Gothic detailing by Augustus Pugin, the Houses of Parliament stand on the site of the medieval Palace of Westminster, destroyed by fire in 1834 (except for Westminster Hall). The clock tower contains the famous bell 'Big Ben', which was named after the first Commissioner of Works, Sir Benjamin Hall. Overleaf: Seen from the South Bank of the Thames at sunset, the Houses of Parliament evoke Britain's long history and the medieval origins of its legislative body.

behind Westminster Hall and next to the clock tower, is approached by Members under the catalpa trees of New Palace Yard. At the far end is the House of Lords. The Royal Entrance is at the extreme south-west corner, under the 50 foot arch of the Victoria Tower. The public entrance is to the left of the arch. Visitors may enter on Saturdays, on some Bank Holidays and on selected days in August and September, to explore the chambers unaccompanied. A flag flying from the Victoria Tower in the daytime indicates that Parliament is sitting.

The chambers are decorated with period furnishing. Traditionally, green is the predominant colour in the Commons chamber and royal red in the Lords, sumptuously decorated in Gothic style by Pugin. The benches of red leather face each other under windows of stained glass. At the south end, within an elaborate gilt canopy, is the Sovereign's Throne. The cushion in front of this is the famous Woolsack. The chambers are linked by a labyrinth of lobbies, staircases and corridors. The Commons was rebuilt after World War II by Sir Giles Gilbert Scott, who followed Sir Winston Churchill's advice and scaled his design so as not to discourage 'conversational style' in debate. A statue of Churchill by Oscar Nemon stands opposite a figure of Lloyd George at the entrance to the Commons.

Westminster Hall, facing New Palace Yard at the northern front of the building, is a medieval survivor of the fire of 1834 and of previous destructive fires. Remodelled for Richard II by Henry Yevele, it is one of the finest and largest timber-roofed buildings in England. It was the chief law court of England from 1224 to 1882 and was the scene of many famous trials, including those of Sir Thomas More and Guy Fawkes and the condemnation of Charles I. Its great oak roof has been described as 'one of the finest feats of carpentry extant'.

In Parliament Square on the north side is Epstein's Field Marshal Smuts, and among other illustrious figures facing the central lawns are Lord Palmerston by Woolner, and Sir Robert Peel and Lord Derby, both by Matthew Noble. Mario Raggi's statue of Benjamin Disraeli is decorated with primroses, his favourite flowers, on 19 April, Primrose Day and the anniversary of Disraeli's death.

Along the west of the square in front of the Middlesex Crown Court is a replica of Gauden's Abraham Lincoln,

given by the people of the United States in 1920, and a statue of George Canning by Sir Richard Westmacott. At the south end of the square, standing in front of Westminster Abbey, is the parish church of Westminster, St Margaret's, which, since 1621, has been the 'national church for the use of the House of Commons'.

St Paul's Cathedral

This triumph of English Renaissance architecture and Sir Christopher Wren's masterpiece, is a symbol of revival and survival to Londoners, and the spiritual heart of the City. The incomparable west front, approached by steps, is double-colonnaded and flanked by towers enriched by sculptures. St Paul's Portland stone was cleaned in 1964 and revealed a mellow white exterior, as well as some hitherto barely discernible carvings. The magnificent dome, 102 feet in diameter, is probably the finest in Europe and miraculously survived World War II bomb damage.

The word, *Resurgam*, in a carving over the south entrance recalls the building of St Paul's Cathedral amid the devastation of the City after the Great Fire of 1666. Wren laid the foundation stone in 1675, on the site of the Norman cathedral, Old St Paul's. Later a workman, directed to find a marker for the positioning of the dome, picked up from the rubble the charred remnant of a gravestone bearing the single word *Resurgam*, 'I shall rise again'.

The vast interior with its soaring piers and arches and with its mosaic and carvings, is lit from the dome through clear glass. The former stained glass was badly damaged in World War II and its simpler replacement is in keeping with Wren's original intentions. The interior of the great dome is decorated with paintings by Sir James Thornhill, finished in 1710.

Grinling Gibbons' exquisite carvings of the organ case and choir stalls can be seen beyond the tracery of gates made by the great eighteenth century ironworker, Jean Tijou. In the choir is the shrouded effigy of the poet, John Donne, which was all that survived the Great Fire, and which bears traces of flames. Above the high altar a carved, gilded canopy commemorates Commonwealth citizens of all creeds who perished in World War II. The memorial to the American fallen is in the Jesus Chapel, which occupies the apse of the Cathedral.

In the crypt, the tombs of Nelson and

ST. PAUL'S CATHEDRAL
Overleaf: Sir Christopher Wren's masterpiece replaced the medieval cathedral, burnt down—along with most of the City of London—in the Great Fire of 1666. The majestic dome, considered by many the finest in Europe, is a triumph of engineering. The exterior shell is made of wood, covered with lead, but it and the stone cupola rest on a masonry cone (a stronger form than a dome). The inner dome—though not nearly so high as the outer one—is impressively lofty. A visit to the Whispering Gallery, which runs around the inside of the cupola, affords a breathtaking view of the interior.

ROYAL FESTIVAL HALL
Built for the Festival of Britain in 1951, the Festival Hall (seen here with the Houses of Parliament in the background) is one of a complex of concert halls and theatres located on the South Bank of the Thames.

Wellington lie near memorials to many of Britain's famous artists, among them Reynolds, Turner and Millais. Among plaques bearing other illustrious names is the poignant tablet of 'an American citizen who died that England might live'. But perhaps the most rewarding is the tablet commemorating Sir Christopher Wren, *si monumentum requiris, circumspice,* 'if you would seek his monument, look around'.

High in the dome are the Whispering Gallery and the library, with Sir Christopher Wren's models of St Paul's Cathedral. These he changed three times before winning approval from the church commissioners whose strictures dogged him from the beginning until the day in 1710 when Sir Christopher Wren, by then an old man, watched his son climb 365 feet to lay the last stone at the summit of the lantern. Visitors who climb the 375 steps to the stone gallery will be rewarded with panoramic views of today's new City.

South Bank

This unique grouping of galleries, theatres and concert halls fronts a paved promenade along the Thames from Hungerford Bridge to Waterloo Bridge. The group incorporates the Royal Festival and Queen Elizabeth Halls, the Hayward Gallery, the National Film Theatre and the National Theatre. The modern structures, mainly of textured concrete, are linked by a series of winding stairways and raised, paved walks.

The first building of the series, the Royal Festival Hall, was constructed and opened as a concert hall for the 1951 Festival of Britain, and extended early in the 1960s. Approached by the Hungerford Bridge, the hall's curved façade, faced with Portland stone, has been praised as one of London's most successful examples of post-war architecture. An expansive window area allows excellent views of the riverside from the restaurants which, with a network of comfortable foyers and bars, encompass the main concert hall. This, with a seating capacity of 3400, with a platform designed to hold a choir of 250, and with its own custom-built organ, is one of the most acoustically accurate concert halls in the world. The building incorporates a ballroom, and the main hall can also be used to stage ballet productions.

Next, down-river, the Queen Elizabeth Hall with seats for an audience of over 1000, is housed in a tiered, square building which was opened in 1967. This incorporates the Purcell Room, where smaller audiences can hear recitals and chamber music. Behind, on a level with Waterloo Bridge, is the Hayward Gallery, also of dark concrete, opened in 1968 for Arts Council exhibitions. Tucked under Waterloo Bridge is the National Film Theatre where members can attend seasons of films classified under period or genre as well as foreign and experimental films of interest to the film enthusiast. The 1980 highlight was *Napoleon*, a 1927 silent epic.

Beyond Waterloo Bridge is the National Theatre, the latest and perhaps most interesting building, opened in 1976. It accommodates the Olivier Theatre with just over 1000 seats, the Lyttleton Theatre for repertory productions, and the small Cottesloe Theatre for experimental work. The building is light-coloured, a series of flat terraces and towers with dark tiled pavements and stairways. Bars, bookshops, buffets and exhibitions are housed within the complex, which is also a venue for musical events and poetry readings.

Between Hungerford Bridge and County Hall is the Shell Centre, which has a handsome lower façade but is otherwise sombre. For a small fee visitors can take in spectacular panoramas of London from the viewing gallery.

Street Markets

London is particularly well-endowed with produce and antique markets. In many areas, one or two days a week, a street is closed to traffic so that stalls offering fruit and vegetables, second-hand goods, china and new or used clothes can sell their wares. Most main markets deal in wholesale goods from the early morning, then stay open for private buyers until midday.

Leadenhall Market, Gracechurch Street, E.C.3 is open on weekday mornings. Once a poultry market, Leadenhall deals in meat, poultry, game and fish, fruit, vegetables and provisions. The market is housed in graceful and elaborately ornamented Victorian arcades, built over a medieval market, which was in turn sited over part of a Roman basilica and forum of A.D. 80–100. Refreshment centres around The Lamb, a pub with upstairs dining rooms.

Camden Passage, Charlton Place is a labyrinth of late Georgian passages and arcades off Upper Street and Essex Road, N.1. Trading takes place mainly on Wednesdays and Saturdays, although

some shops are open in usual business hours throughout the week. This flourishing centre for a wide range of antiques and bric-à-brac deals predominantly in Victorian ware. Many stalls and shops specialize in particular fields, such as paintings and watercolours, silver, Victorian toys, papier-mâché and clocks. Some stalls also carry modern crafts. Wholesale trading starts at 7.30 a.m. on Wednesdays but Saturday is the most popular day for the casual buyer. There are a number of interesting pubs, wine bars, coffee shops and restaurants near by.

The Bermondsey Antique Market, Long Lane, S.E.1 extends east in to The New Caledonian Market in Abbey Street. Both markets open only on Fridays, the former for the morning, the latter all day. These markets deal solely in antiques, mainly Victorian silver, brassware, china and furniture, jewellery and household goods. Collectors and dealers arrive at dawn in summer and before dawn in winter to do business with specialists. By law, purchases can be made only during daylight hours, so in winter the goods are selected, a price agreed, and the purchase reserved. Plenty is left for the private buyer after the dealers have departed around 9 a.m. Breakfast can be enjoyed at one of the many cafés in the area, or in one of the pubs, several of which are licensed to sell drinks from 7.30 a.m. on market day.

One of London's most famous markets is Portobello Road, W.11. The road itself runs from Pembridge Villas to Golborne Road and the market's main trading day is Saturday. Different sections of Portobello deal in different commodities, but this is one of London's major antique and specialist centres. From the Pembridge Villas end, Portobello offers general antiques and furniture, prints, paintings, miniatures, Oriental or European porcelain, feathers, fans, cutlery, walking sticks and a variety of other collectors' items. Mixed in with these, valuable military uniforms, T-shirts and craft-work are offered for sale. From Elgin Terrace northward the stalls deal in fruit and vegetables and are open on weekdays. Farther north near Lancaster Road a confusing mixture of stalls offer cheap bric-à-brac, junk furniture, household equipment, and second-hand clothes. The market ends with a cosmopolitan, West Indian flavour around Golborne Road. Throughout the market pubs, restaurants, hot-dog stalls, buskers and street musicians abound.

Petticoat Lane, Middlesex Street, E.1 which is open on Sunday mornings from about 8 a.m. to midday, was for a long time London's most famous flea market. This market deals almost solely in new commodities and is worth visiting for the diversity of its wares as well as its stallholders and customers. Whole stalls are devoted to the sale of cashew nuts, or of umbrellas, cloth caps, digital watches, bananas or chamois leather. A stall displaying kosher poultry is next to a winkle stall on one side and a barrow stacked with suitcases on another. Across the street a stallholder demonstrates gyroscopes while his neighbour wraps an electro-plated coffee service for a customer.

This seething complex is contained by main lorry routes and areas undergoing development. Close by is the Houndsditch Warehouse, a Sunday hypermarket and across the busy streets are other Sunday street markets specializing in plants, pets and second-hand goods.

Tower Bridge

One of London's most powerful landmarks, Tower Bridge symbolizes the interdependence between city and river. It is the last of the downstream bridges, and its 1100 ton bascules are raised by electric motors to allow tall vessels through to the Inner Pool of London. The bascules, once opened several times a day, can be raised in one and a half minutes, although they are rarely drawn to their full height. This is only done as a gesture of honour and respect for illustrious visitors. Sir Francis Chichester, when he returned from his round the world voyage in 1967, was so honoured.

The bridge carries South London traffic to the Tower of London, which stands on the waterside immediately to the west. To the east, on the other side of Tower Bridge Approach, is the yachting marina and pleasure area, St Katherine's Dock. An Act of Parliament gives river traffic absolute precedence over road traffic. A telephone message from Cherry Garden Pier, Bermondsey, advises the Bridge Master of vessels approaching from downstream and a watchman on the bridge keeps a constant look out for vessels approaching from London Bridge. The morse signal for the letter 'B', a long blast and three short blasts, sounded on the ship's siren and accompanied by hoisting a black ball and pennant at the forestay, is the correct request for the bascules to be raised. A staff of some 80 men assist the Bridge Master in raising

TOWER BRIDGE
Above: This famous bridge was opened in 1894. Within its two towers is machinery for raising and lowering the drawbridges to permit ships to pass through.

Overleaf: Tower Bridge looking downstream. About 10,000 vehicles cross the bridge every day.

the bridge and general maintenance.

The bridge's twin towers linked by latticework footbridges high over the main span give it a medieval appearance, which was the intention of the War Office who commissioned its design in the 1880s from Sir John Barry and Sir Horace Jones. To make the bridge even more in keeping with its surroundings, close to the Tower of London, Sir Horace proposed that the bascules should be raised by means of massive chains. After his death the idea was abandoned, and power was supplied by hydraulic pumps until 1975. The bridge, built between 1886 and 1894 at a cost of £800,000, is constructed of steel covered with brickwork and faced with granite. 'Steel skeletons clothed in stone', was the comment of the architects. The central span, 800 feet in length between its massive towers, stands $29\frac{1}{2}$ feet above high water and carries an estimated 10,000 vehicles daily. The footbridges, 142 feet above high water level, were closed before World War I because of the practical problem of policing difficulties. The City of London, however, is now making moves to reopen the footbridges as a public way.

The Tower of London

This is the oldest and largest continuously occupied fortress in the western world, and one of the few to remain unconquered. It comprises 18 acres of towers, extensions and fortifications added in every century until the present. The Norman White Tower which forms the central keep, was begun by the prudent William the Conqueror as a fortress from which to control London. It was completed about 1097 by William II. In the thirteenth century Henry III strengthened the Tower by adding two lines of wall around the keep, and it was he who decorated the interior to make it a gracious palace. Henry's son Edward I, among other improvements between 1275 and 1285, installed the grim stone arch and iron grill later to be known as 'Traitors' Gate' where, in the sixteenth and seventeenth centuries, illustrious prisoners were brought by barge to the dungeons straight from Westminster.

It is as a state prison, rather than as a fort or palace, that the Tower is best known. Yet it once housed the Royal Mint and an Observatory, and from Henry III's reign until Victorian times

the Tower contained a menagerie which was removed to Regent's Park Zoo in 1834. But for visitors who tour the towers and grounds, associations of imprisonment, torture, murder and execution are inescapable. The murder of the little Princess in the Tower in 1483 is of dubious authenticity; but famous 'traitors' such as Sir Thomas More, Guy Fawkes, Sir Walter Raleigh and Elizabeth I's favourite, the Earl of Essex, were executed here, as were two of Henry VIII's queens, Anne Boleyn and Catherine Howard. Here also the seventeen-year-old Lady Jane Grey, queen of England for nine days, was sent with her husband to the scaffold by her cousin, Mary Tudor (Bloody Mary). In the infamous Bloody Tower more than 90 prisoners have inscribed their signatures on the wall.

Today, visitors can examine the magnificent display of medieval armoury in the White Tower. The Waterloo Barracks, built by the Duke of Wellington in 1845, house the priceless and heavily-guarded Crown Jewels. At 9.40 p.m. when the Tower is floodlit, visitors who have applied to the Resident Governor can witness the ancient Ceremony of the Keys, when the main gates are locked. The traditional overseers of the Tower are not only the sinister ravens but the splendid Yeoman Warders, the Beefeaters, who still wear Tudor dress. According to legend, when the ravens disappear the Tower will fall down.

On the gentle heights of Tower Hill souvenirs and ice creams are sold and holiday crowds can watch escapologists and other impromptu players. The Tower also has a series of pleasant walks. Along the riverside are a number of cannon captured at Waterloo and along the foreshore of the river is a playbeach for children. The church of All-Hallows-by-the-Tower nearby has a Saxon arch, which was revealed by bomb damage. The church was carefully restored in 1958 and the original brick tower, which survived the Fire of London, is the only example of Cromwellian church architecture in London.

Waterside Pubs Down-River

From the Anchor Inn on Bankside in Southwark to the Trafalgar Tavern down-river at Greenwich, some interesting pubs remain along London's once-flourishing dockside. Most were established before the wharves and warehouses were built, and they prospered from the docks' trade through the

nineteenth and early twentieth centuries. Now, incorporated into new development plans, many have been restored and their low ceilings, oak beams and small crowded bars give the same sense of continuity as the Thames flowing alongside.

The Anchor, facing the site of the old Clink Prison, was built five years before the prison was burned in 1780 by the Gordon Rioters. Upstairs from the restaurant are fine views across the river.

The George Inn, Borough High Street, Southwark, is now the only galleried inn surviving in London and the last of many famous taverns that lined the High Street's approach to London Bridge. One side of the gallery remains and this dates from just after the great Southwark Fire of 1676. The Inn is now the property of the National Trust.

The Angel, Rotherhithe Street, next to the King's Stair Gardens (a stretch of green along the riverside), has a fine view from its enclosed wood balcony over the water. It was built in 1682 and frequented by Samuel Pepys and Captain Cook.

The Mayflower, once the Spread Eagle but renamed in 1957, stands opposite St Mary's Church in Rotherhithe Street. It has the distinction of being the only restaurant and inn with a franchise to sell postage stamps. Its small platform jutting over the Thames is reached through a crowded bar, low-beamed, dark and polished. The Mayflower is reputed to be the embarkation point of the Pilgrim Fathers in 1620. The grave of the *Mayflower*'s captain, Christopher Jones, lies in the tree-shaded churchyard outside. The warehouses round about have been refurbished for use as craft workshops, and other fine buildings of the eighteenth and nineteenth centuries have been restored.

Across the river in Wapping High Street is the famous Prospect of Whitby, said to have been a smuggling inn. It was built in the seventeenth century when Wapping was the domain of pirates and cut-throats. The bars are crowded and the view from the platform where Turner and Whistler painted the river is particularly fine. Pepys is said to have frequented the restaurant upstairs. Other historic pubs in this area include the Town of Ramsgate near Wapping Old Stairs, which has a pleasant Snug Bar, and The Grapes at Limehouse, visited by Dickens while he was working on *Our Mutual Friend*.

At Greenwich is the Trafalgar Tavern,

THE TOWER OF LONDON AND TOWER BRIDGE
Overleaf: A fine view of two of London's best known land marks. The stone monument in front of the castle moat (foreground) is a memorial to British merchant seamen killed in World Wars I and II.

THE TOWER OF LONDON
Right: The oldest part of the Tower—called the White Tower because it was whitewashed—this Norman keep was completed in 1097. It served as a royal residence, as well as a fortress and prison. Ironically, the first prisoner confined within its massive walls—the Bishop of Durham—managed to escape; later inmates were not so fortunate. Today the White Tower houses an impressive collection of armour, including a suit made for Henry VIII. The neighbouring Jewel House contains the Crown Jewels.

which dates from 1837 and was once famous for its whitebait and oysters. The fine building with bowed windows and balconies rises straight from the river. It was restored in the 1960s, and its dining rooms and bars returned to their former splendour.

At the Cutty Sark, farther along the waterfront, whitebait is still served in the dining room upstairs. This is a small old pub dating from 1801 with wood panelling inside. It is a free house and a proper 'local'. Outside, wooden benches look out to Limehouse, across the river.

Westminster Abbey

Westminster Abbey, built from the thirteenth to the sixteenth centuries, is one of Britain's most glorious churches.

Legend ascribes to the site a Roman temple and a Saxon Church. The present Abbey was begun in 1245 by Henry III as a memorial to Edward the Confessor on the site of Edward's church, part of the Benedictine abbey founded before in the eighth century to the west of the City of London (hence Westminster). Henry pulled it down, to rebuild a more fitting and magnificent shrine to the saint. His superb choir and transepts, the harmonious proportions showing French Gothic influence, are the earliest parts of the main body of the church. Work continued for three centuries after Henry's death in 1272, with the great architect Henry Yevele rebuilding portions of the nave, taller than any other English Cathedral, about 1388. Henry VII's Chapel, with its incomparable and

LONDON PUBS
One of the most characteristic features of the English scene, pubs offer a convivial atmosphere for enjoying a drink and a chat with friends. Some of London's most historic pubs can be found along the Thames.
Above: The Mayflower, located in Rotherhithe, on the south bank of the river.
Right: The Prospect of Whitby, on the north bank, a favourite with tourists and locals, too.

intricate vaulting, was added to the east of Edward the Confessor's sanctuary between 1503 and 1509.

The exterior of the abbey has been much worked on, and the western towers were added in 1734 by Wren's pupil Nicholas Hawksmoor.

Entering the west door, the visitor is confronted with an interior of stunning beauty. The white arcades, the gilt touches in the roof far overhead, the dark columns of Purbeck marble, the tracery of Henry VII's roof at the far end and the curved clerestory, create an unforgettable impact. The tomb of the Unknown Warrior, set into the floor some little way inside, and the plain marble slab inscribed 'Remember Winston Churchill' a few steps over the threshold, are appropriate in their simplicity.

As Britain's most illustrious resting place, the Abbey houses innumerable memorials and tombs. Musicians' Corner can be seen in the north aisle of the choir. In the south transept, Poets' Corner commemorates major writers and poets, including Geoffrey Chaucer, Shakespeare, Charles Dickens, Rudyard Kipling and many others.

In the most sacred part of the Abbey,

the Sanctuary, is the shrine of Edward the Confessor, mutilated during the Reformation. Here, too, is the oak coronation chair, made by Walter of Durham in 1300 and one of the most famous pieces of furniture in the world; and the Stone of Scone with its inscription 'If Fates go right, where e'er this stone is found, the Scots shall monarch of that realm be crowned'. Here the coronation of every English monarch since William I's time, with the exception of Edward V and Edward VIII, has taken place.

Beyond the High Altar, which is a reproduction of the famous Florentine sculptor, Torrigiano's magnificent original, is Edward the Confessor's Chapel, the 'burial place of kings', where England's Kings and Queens were interred until the reign of George III. In Henry VII's exquisite chapel are the banners of the Knights of the Bath hung above many tombs, notably those of Elizabeth I and her sister Mary. The chapel also contains Torrigiano's magnificent black marble tomb for Henry VII made in 1509. Here Henry lies with his wife Elizabeth of York, who died in childbirth in 1503, three weeks after the first stone of Henry's chapel was laid.

WESTMINSTER ABBEY
Above: Henry VII's Chapel, one of the finest examples of English Perpendicular Gothic, is located behind the High Altar and contains the tombs of Henry, the first Tudor king, and his Queen, Elizabeth of York. Right: The West Front. Although the Abbey was built mainly in the thirteenth century, it has subsequently been added to and restored. The two western towers were added in the eighteenth century by Hawksmoor.

Ireland

Dunluce Castle on the Atlantic shores of County Antrim.

Bantry House and Bay

Bantry Bay is a long, broad inlet of the sea facing south-westwards on the Atlantic coast of County Cork. Washed by the Gulf Stream the whole region is famous for its mild climate and the luxuriant growth of flowers and shrubs that thrive there. The deep waters of the Bay make Bantry Harbour a natural visiting point for Spanish and French fishing fleets, and more than once in the past the walls of the little port have rung with the cannon-fire of foreign warships.

Bantry House stands on the south shores of the bay facing across the inlet to the Caha Mountains. Built for the Hutchinson family in the 1740s, it was soon acquired by the prosperous Richard White who moved to the house in 1765. White's son, another Richard, won the approval of the English by his nimble presence of mind when the French fleet appeared in Bantry Bay in December 1796. His 'zeal and loyalty' earned him the title of Earl of Bantry.

The house is open to the public daily, except on Saturdays. Inside and out it is a successful blend of styles. On to the square three-storeyed structure of the original building have been added a wing

of late eighteenth century date, and a remodelled south front (about 1840). This nineteenth century addition was the work of the second Earl, and some important items from his collections are on view. The oldest objects are two tablets from Pompeii inscribed 'cave canem' and 'salve'. Fine Dutch and French tapestries decorate the walls, and the Italian gardens of the house are renowned.

On the north side of Bantry Bay lies the famous village of Glengariff. Of all the burgeoning shores of County Cork Glengariff's are the mildest and their vegetation the most profuse. Fuschia, holly, and other species abound even to the water's edge. This richness of plant life has made Glengariff a popular resort, particularly for winter holidays. A rewarding excursion is the short boat trip from Glengariff harbour to the lovely gardens of Garinish Island, laid out as a paradise of temples, shrubberies and trees. Many of the species are of Mediterranean and subtropical origins, flourishing far from their native soil. Garinish Island is now owned by the State, and has special associations with George Bernard Shaw who wrote much of St Joan here.

BANTRY HOUSE
Above: The home of the Earls of Bantry dates from 1740, though much of it, including the 14-bay south front, was added later. It contains a fine collection of paintings and furniture.

STORMONT, NORTHERN IRELAND
Right: Located just outside Belfast, the Stormont estate is the seat of government for Northern Ireland. This neo-classical building, constructed in 1928, houses the province's parliament, now disbanded as a result of the 'troubles'.

Belfast

Belfast, the capital of the North and the second largest city in Ireland, sits at the estuary of the River Lagan on the wide coastal inlet of Belfast Lough. Though the river-crossing at this point has given significance to the site from the Stone Age onwards, the modern city is the product of the Industrial Revolution, retaining few reminders of its earlier roles.

1177 is the most important date in the early history of Belfast. In this year the invading forces of John de Courcy destroyed the existing fort at Beal-feirste 'the sandy ford', and established a Norman castle which was later to form the nucleus of a small town. Both town and castle were to be sacked by Edward Bruce in 1316, but the commercial and strategic importance of Belfast's position was now established, and for the next 300 years its fortunes were to reflect the intermittent struggle for the control of Northern Ireland.

In 1603 Sir Arthur Chichester obtained a grant of the region from James I, and after this date it is possible to trace the first hesitant steps in Belfast's commercial growth. A royal charter of 1613 gave the town the status of a Parliamentary borough, and from 1685 onwards the industrious Huguenots added their energy and skill to Belfast's expanding trade, so that by the middle of the eighteenth century visitors were commenting on the prosperity and elegance of Belfast.

The speed of Belfast's industrial expansion can be judged from the growth of population. In 1750 there were 8500 inhabitants. In 1800 there were 20,000. Eighty years later the numbers had expanded more than ten-fold, and today the population is little short of half a million people. Against such a pattern of enlargement few cities could preserve their heritage intact. Compensation can best be found in the collections and public buildings.

Architecturally the main features of modern Belfast owe much to the work of two men. Roger Mulholland working in the late eighteenth century established the regular street plan which was to give symmetry to the town's later expansion. Sir Charles Lanyon (1813–1889) designed many of the finest buildings of the city between 1840 and 1860. Among the best of these are Queen's University, the Customs House, the Presbyterian Assembly Buildings and the distinguished offices of the Northern Bank.

Sir Brumwell Thomas's City Hall and the Royal Academical Institution.

The dual function of Art Gallery and Museum are conveniently united in the Ulster Museum on the southern edge of central Belfast. Works by Turner, Lawrence, Wilson and Sickert are among the many exhibits. Natural history, archaeology and technology are also admirably represented. Near by the 40 acres of the Botanic Gardens, stretching from University Road to the banks of the Lagan, are a credit to the Municipality.

In spite of the size of their city Belfast people are never far from the countryside. The southern end of the Lough is ringed by green hills, charming in themselves and full of interest for the inquisitive visitor. Hilltop forts from the Stone Age and Iron Age are plentiful in this region and Cave Hill, 1182 feet high and close to the nineteenth century walls of Belfast Castle commands an impressive view of the coastline.

Carrickfergus Castle

Carrickfergus Castle is probably the most complete medieval fortress in Ireland. Towering above the small town and harbour the castle's fortunes have for centuries been bound up with the stormy history of Ireland.

Little is known of the earliest days of this 'Rock of Fergus', so called after the powerful King Fergus MacErc whose death by shipwreck in Belfast Lough occurred in 320. However, the name is unlikely to be purely commemorative and it is probable that the military vantage-point of Carrickfergus was already in use as a royal demesne at the close of the third century. The Anglo-Norman invaders of 1177 seized upon the site as a bastion from which to push forward their conquests into Antrim, and within 20 years of the foundation of the Norman Keep it had already been twice besieged. Of the many generals who were to blockade Carrickfergus in the course of its long history Hugh de Lacy, King John, Edward Bruce and William III's General Schomberg are the most prominent. As late as 1760 it was stormed – and briefly taken – by the French in a surprise raid, and Carrickfergus was not finally to cease its military duties until the present century, after a serving life of 750 years.

The castle is open to the public daily throughout the year. It houses a museum of antiquities including collections of uniforms and armour, prints and medals. The old portcullis and the mechanism

ST. ANNE'S CATHEDRAL, BELFAST
This Protestant cathedral was begun in 1898. Its façade shows the influence of Norman, or Romanesque, architecture.

which raised it are also preserved in the Gate Tower. But by far the finest antiquity is the castle itself: starting from the Inner Ward on the south side the visitor may study the development of the fortifications from the original five-storey Keep of about 1180, through three stages of outer walls, until the perimeter defence-works occupy the whole rock. The Great Hall on the third floor of the Keep and the vista from the fourth floor should certainly be enjoyed.

Beneath the castle, the town of Carrickfergus – once the greatest seaport in Northern Ireland – accepts its altered status with dignity. The church of St Nicholas, the oldest part dating from the twelfth century, contains some interesting Jacobean work. The North Gate of the town and a section of the town's walls are also preserved.

The naval engagement between the victorious John Paul Jones's *Ranger* and *HMS Drake* took place off Carrickfergus in 1778.

Castletownshend Village

The village of Castletownshend between Clonakilty and Skibbereen offers a charming blend of beauty, history and literary associations that is seldom found in such a small community. Set amid countryside which is lovely even by the standards of County Cork the walks around the village are enhanced by their connections with the past.

'The Fort', on Knockdown Hill northwest of Castletownshend, is a well-preserved stone ring-fort, now maintained as a National Monument, with ramparts and guard chambers still intact. Nearby is an interesting Stone Age formation of pillars known as the Three Fingers, and to the north-east of the village the seventeenth century remains of Bryan's Fort saw action in the campaign of 1688–1689.

These focal points are all an easy walking distance from Castletownshend. Along the same paths, after the death of his beloved Vanessa, Dean Swift would wander during the summer of 1723, bereft, but still writing of the Ireland he loved.

A more recent link with the literature of Ireland is Drishane House on the southern edge of Castletownshend. It was here that Edith Somerville, joint author of *Some Experiences of an Irish RM* lived and wrote many of her books. A spiritualist and an eccentric, Edith Somerville's work was criticized during her lifetime as nihilistic: to the ardent

advocates of the new republic her humorous tales of a Resident Magistrate often seemed retrogressive, but the continuing popularity of her writing 30 years after her death at the age of 91 is testimony to the resilience of her art.

Edith Somerville's collaborator 'Martin Ross' was in fact her friend Violet Martin. Violet died in 1915, but Edith Somerville maintained that her later books were still jointly written thanks to her continuing spiritual contact with her friend. The two lie buried in St Barrahane's Church, and Edith Somerville's house remains in the possession of her family.

Dublin

Dublin was first mentioned by the geographer Ptolemy in the year A.D. 140 when he referred to it as 'Eblana'. Eleven hundred years ago the longboats of the Scandinavian invaders nosed into the quiet waters of the Liffey and beached beside the shallow crossing of Baile Atha Cliath. Here they built a camp, settled, and extended the site until it grew into a flourishing town, Dubh Linn (Dark Pool) as it came to be known in Gaelic.

Dublin at first was little more than one of a number of coastal stations established by the Norse pirates. However, its central position astride land and water routes gave the settlement a pre-eminence in Ireland which was never to falter, and after the expulsion of the Vikings from Dublin by Henry II of England in 1171 it became the seat of government for lands controlled by the Anglo-Norman barons. A cluster of Norman fortresses around the capital protected the governed area against attack from beyond the Pale.

Today a few important monuments still survive from this early period. The oldest of them all – and a source of controversy to Dubliners over the last few years – are the archaeological remains of a Viking quay and other buildings on the south bank of the Liffey immediately to the west of Christchurch Cathedral. These finds have been made very recently and it will be some years before they can be fully excavated and displayed. Civic plans to remove the remains from their original site have been vigorously resisted.

Towering above the scene of these excavations, Christchurch Cathedral is the oldest standing structure in Dublin. It was founded by a Dane, the Christianized Viking leader Sigfrig 'Silken-

CASTLETOWNSHEND VILLAGE
Overleaf: Fish baskets on the quay of one of County Cork's most attractive and historic villages. In these waters (Castlehaven) a Spanish squadron was annihilated during a three-day battle with English warships (1601).

CARRICKFERGUS CASTLE
Right: The best-preserved Norman fortress in Ireland, Carrickfergus has, however, seen some bloody battles. In 1689, held by forces loyal to James II, it finally fell to William III's army after heavy bombardment. The town, about 11 miles from Belfast, was once an important port. Here the American naval captain John Paul Jones defeated a British warship during the American War of Independence.

beard' in 1038. The cathedral was substantially restored in the nineteenth century by George Edmund Street, but it retains strong connections with an earlier benefactor Richard de Clare, nicknamed Strongbow, the leader of the Anglo-Norman force that first captured the city. As a counterbalance to the influence of Strongbow and his party the neighbouring Cathedral of St Patrick was established by Archbishop John Comyn in 1190 by enlarging the ancient Church of St Patrick de Insula. The pleasing structure of St Patrick's contains a rich profusion of monuments including a bust and tablet of its most famous dean, Jonathan Swift (1667–1745).

Dublin Castle, overlooking the river to the East of the two cathedrals, is the third of the city's great medieval structures. Started in 1204 the castle has seen service as fortress, prison, palace and records office – often serving several of these functions at once. The styles of architecture within the castle are appropriately diverse. The staterooms are open to visitors, and the throne room, picture gallery, and genealogical office are of particular interest.

But it is to the eighteenth century that we must look for the greater glories of Dublin. These glories are not to be found only in the magnificent architecture of the city; the squares and buildings of Dublin are just one expression of a wider flowering of genius never surpassed by a city of comparable size. From the age of Swift onwards for 70 years the capital drew to itself an aristocracy of wealth and intelligence, pre-eminent in many fields; Richard Steele, Richard Brinsley Sheridan, Thomas Moore, John Field, Henry Grattan, James Napper Tandy, Theobald Wolfe Tone, Robert Emmet, Edmund Burke, Arthur Wellesley, Duke of Wellington – these are only a few of Dublin's eighteenth century sons.

The thriving life and aspirations of Dublin society today are very different from the privileged world of the eighteenth century. Yet the city's artistic achievements abound as strongly as ever. A handful of names – Oscar Wilde, George Bernard Shaw, J. M. Synge, Sean O'Casey, James Joyce, Samuel Beckett, Brendan Behan – will suffice to show the continuity of the tradition. For the visitor, the fine buildings that surround him, many now receiving a much-needed restoration, enhance his appreciation of a city which offers so much more than its own elegance.

College Green boasts the greatest concentration of Classical architecture. Here, across the bustling thoroughfare, the lordly colonnades of the Bank of Ireland, formerly Grattan's Parliament, gaze serenely out on to the grand portico of Trinity College's West Front. Trinity, founded in 1591, contains few surviving Tudor structures, most of the older buildings having been demolished or incorporated into the scheme of formal quadrangles by a succession of eighteenth century architects. The Old Library, for example, dates from 1712 to 1732, although the collection which it houses was begun over a century before. Since 1801 Trinity Library has been one of the four copyright libraries entitled to a free copy of every book published in the British Isles. Its greatest treasure is the Book of Kells, an early ninth century manuscript of the gospels, richly illustrated, and one of the triumphs of early Irish art. The library and grounds of Trinity College are open to the public.

Like all modern capitals Dublin has attractions to suit a variety of tastes. Its hotels, offices and restaurants bustle with the activity of an expanding economy. Grafton Street is famous for its elegant shops, and the Abbey Theatre, rebuilt on the site made famous by Yeats, has productions which are internationally acclaimed. Those with an interest in the arts will find the National Gallery of Ireland, the National Museum, and the Chester Beatty Library and Gallery of Oriental Art to be among the best of their type in the world.

For specialist interests Guinness's Brewery, the complex now covering over 60 acres, has its main entrance in St James' Gate. Tours of the Brewery itself have been discontinued, but visitors are received nearby in Crane Street to sample the products and to see films of the brewing process. The Royal Dublin Society's showground at Ballsbridge, south-east of the central city area is the scene of the famous Dublin Horse Show.

Dunluce Castle

Dunluce Castle, standing on a rocky promontory about three miles west of Portrush in County Antrim, has one of the most turbulent histories of all the medieval fortresses of Ireland. At a time when most of the great castles of Britain were beginning their slow transformation into country houses the clash of arms still rang around Dunluce's embattled walls.

DUNLUCE CASTLE
Overleaf: Its dramatic location is one outstanding feature of Dunluce, which dates back to 1300, though it was extensively rebuilt in the sixteenth and seventeenth centuries. Today, most of the castle is in ruins—a reflection of the violence that has marked its long history.

ST. PATRICK'S CATHEDRAL, DUBLIN Right: Dating from the twelfth and thirteenth centuries, St. Patrick's became an Anglican cathedral during the long period of British rule of Ireland. Its most illustrious Dean was Jonathan Swift, who served here in the early 1700s. During this period an enormous amount of building took place in Dublin, leaving the city with a rich heritage of Palladian architecture.

'Dunluce' means 'the stronghold'. The first fortifications were probably built on this coastal site by Richard de Burgh, Earl of Ulster, between 1240 and 1320. By the close of the sixteenth century, however, changes in military technique called for a complete rebuilding, with the result that few features of the earlier structure now survive. The present castle, probably built by James MacDonnell about 1590, makes use of local basalt columns from the nearby Giant's Causeway, and the unique formation of these rocks gives the doors and windows an individuality which defies precise dating.

Central to the history of Dunluce is the Scottish family of MacDonnell who pursued their territorial ambitions against Irish and English claimants through several generations. Between 1513 and 1558 the MacDonnells dispossessed the local MacQuillans from the suzerainty of the castle after a number of bloody encounters. Within a few years, however, they themselves were expelled by the redoubtable Shane O'Neill who boasted to his English allies that he had 'kylled and banished all the Skottes out of the North'. In fact this episode was only the start of a new series of butcheries. With an energy and bravura that have become legendary the head of the clan Sorley Boye ('swarthy Charles') MacDonnell wrested back his birthright, and after a lifetime of vicissitudes passed his inheritance to his son James, whose heir Randall MacDonnell was eventually confirmed in his power by the English crown and created Earl of Antrim in 1620.

The fine towers, a barbican, and part of the great hall are the principal survivals of this once mighty fortress. Later additions were constructed on the mainland sometime after 1639 when part of the kitchens collapsed during a dinner party killing eight servants. Between the older and newer parts a sheer gulf 100 feet deep provides a spectacular natural moat. The perilous drawbridge has long since been replaced by a permanent crossing but, once over the chasm, the visitor will find the spell of the haunted Banshee Tower still undiminished.

Giant's Causeway

'Sir,' said Boswell to Dr Johnson on 12 October 1779, 'is not the Giant's Causeway worth seeing?' 'Worth seeing, sir?' exclaimed the sage. 'Yes. But not worth the going to see.'

The best defence for the Doctor's dismissiveness is that he had little knowledge of his subject. From the mid-eighteenth century onwards a succession of discerning visitors to this remarkable natural phenomenon have declared it to be among the wonders of the world. Yet one thing should be said in Johnson's support. The name of the Giant's Causeway is misleading: though surrounded by beetling cliffs and frequently wracked by storms, the Causeway itself is relatively small, and – to those who expect to encounter titanic size – initially disappointing. In the end it is not the size but the sheer precision and quantity of the Causeway's pillars which seize the imagination of all who come here.

The Giant's Causeway stands on the coastal boundary between Londonderry and Antrim about five miles north-west of Dunluce Castle, a fortress partly built from the pillars of the Causeway. Mythologically the Causeway has been linked with Fingal's Cave in the Isle of Staffa, for legend has it that Finn MacCoul the High King of Ulster built the Causeway so that he might walk dry-shod to Scotland. Geologists now know that these two natural features do in fact lie at either end of the same fault in the earth's crust.

The rocks of the Giant's Causeway are made of basalt. During the Cainozoic period – over 50 million years ago – lava burst through the earth's surface and, cooling rapidly, solidified into numberless many-sided columns. Hexagonal columns are most common, but the 'cloghans' (stepping stones) include pillars of between three and nine sides.

The area has been open to visitors since 1963. The 40,000 pillars which make up the Causeway average about 15 inches in diameter and form themselves into three groups, The Little Causeway, The Honeycomb and The Grand Causeway which protrudes over 600 feet into the sea. Particular rocks and groupings such as the Chair, the Giant's Amphitheatre, the Mitre and other imaginative titles are used by geologists and local guides alike.

The best starting point for the Giant's Causeway is from Portnabo (the Crow's Bay) where there is an Information Centre, a tourist shop, and tea rooms. Boats can also be hired here to tour the neighbouring caves of Portcoon – dramatically coloured – and Runkerry, 700 feet long and 60 feet high. A fine general view is obtainable from the nearby headland of Aird Snout.

GIANT'S CAUSEWAY
Irish mythology maintains that this extraordinary natural formation was built by Finn MacCoul, the High King of Ulster, so that he might walk dry-shod to Scotland. It is not so large as its name suggests, but the precision of the faceted stones—mostly hexagonal— is impressive.

123

Glendalough

The ancient ruins of Glendalough, nestling in the Wicklow Mountains some 25 miles south of Dublin, form one of the finest of Ireland's ecclesiastical sites.

The earliest foundation on this secluded spot is attributed to St Kevin late in the sixth century. Trained in the ascetic traditions of the Celtic Church, Kevin, one of the princes of the royal house of Leinster, first dwelt here as a hermit in a cave which now bears his name. His original church, Temple-na-Skellig, The Church of the Rocks, was established high up in the valley, but as the site expanded new structures were added, until by St Kevin's death in 618 the glen was studded with the buildings of a flourishing community.

It is characteristic of Celtic Christianity that a place so remote should be chosen as an ecclesiastical centre. Equally characteristic is the proliferation of small churches, often standing close together in clusters, which abound here. We cannot know for certain how these churches were used, but the probability is that they were the permanent framework of a larger complex of dormitories and halls which have long since vanished. The presence of a royal graveyard at Glendalough points to its importance in the life of Ireland from an early date.

Of the many buildings in the valley the sturdy oratory called St Kevin's Kitchen is one of the simplest and best preserved. This is not, in fact, a kitchen but a church; its name derives from the number of domestic implements found here during restoration. The economy of this ninth century construction is impressive. The walls are low, the roof steeply pitched and secured inside by bracing members which divide the interior into a lower chamber and a loft. The original entrance in the west wall has now been blocked up, and the round bell-tower is of rather later construction than the main building.

Glendalough is rich in recumbent stones. Unlike the stones at Clonmacnois, the ancient gravemarkers here still lie where they were originally placed, their carvings and inscriptions staring upward as the pious hands that laid them from the seventh century onwards intended. A more remarkable group of stones are the bullauns, sometimes called 'the pillows of the saints'. These mysterious relics, unique to Celtic church sites, have bewildered scholars for many years. In their commonest form the bullauns are large boulders, unworked except for an oval or circular hollow which is about nine inches deep. Legend has it that St Kevin used to milk a white doe at the bullaun near St Saviour's church in the lower valley.

Jerpoint Abbey

The Cistercian abbey, Jerpoint, is two miles south-east of Thomastown in the peaceful countryside of County Kilkenny. Built from the plentiful limestone of the region, and endowed by successive generations of the Butler family, the magnificent remains of this once-prosperous foundation contain some of the best works of Irish medieval sculpture.

Jerpoint was originally a Benedictine Abbey, founded by Donagh MacGillapatrick, King of Ossory, in 1158. The present plan of the buildings, however, is typical of the Cistercians whose contemplative life, allied to their traditional interests in sheep farming, encouraged them to colonize and extend the site. Clairvaux Abbey was a parent house of Jerpoint, and Fountains Abbey in Yorkshire one of a number of sister foundations. After the Dissolution of the Monasteries Jerpoint was leased to the Earls of Ormonde.

In outline the Abbey's buildings are grouped around a central quadrangle. The north side of this cloister is occupied by the triple-aisled church, while the domestic offices of the community, kitchens, dormitories, and chapterhouse, flank the other sides. The piers of the cloister arcade are now largely restored and contain outstanding examples of fifteenth century decoration.

Within the church there are a number of survivals from Jerpoint's earliest period. The east end, with the exception of the fourteenth century each window, dates from the 1160s. The nave is somewhat later, its north wall in particular being constructed during the extensive alterations of the fifteenth century. Part of the south aisle, and the tower with its stepped battlements, characteristic of Irish church architecture in this period, also stem from the high days of the fifteenth century woollen trade. The original great altar now stands in the Catholic church at Thomastown.

Jerpoint's monuments are particularly impressive. In the Choir stands the tomb of Felix O'Dullany, Bishop of Ossory (1178–1202). It was the energetic leadership of Bishop Felix which first brought Jerpoint into prominence,

KNOCK
Overleaf: The tiny village of Knock became world-famous when Pope John Paul II visited it in 1979, the centenary of the appearance of the Virgin Mary to worshippers at its parish church, shown here. The shrine attracts pilgrims from many nations.

JERPOINT ABBEY
Left: The ruins of this twelfth century Cistercian abbey are ornamented with some of the finest Irish medieval sculpture, including distinctive tomb effigies of saints and nobles.

and the spiritual battle which he fought is vividly displayed on his tomb by a combat between the Serpent and the Cross. The fifteenth century tombs of the Walsh and Butler families adorn the south transept. The Walshes were the ancient seneschals of Leinster, one of whom, Thomas Fitzanthony Walsh, constructed the castle and walls of Thomastown. But the most striking monuments are the effigies of a knight and his lady, probably representing Peter Butler (d 1493) and his wife Isabella Blanchfield.

Kerry

The 'Ring of Kerry' is perhaps the most famous of Irish tours and stretches 112 miles following the coastline of the Iveragh Peninsula in the south-west, providing views of some of the most breathtaking scenery in Ireland. The standard route is to begin from Killorglin and work down through the lakes and mountains of the area, across the foot of the peninsula and, finally, back up in a north-easterly direction to Kenmare and then Killarney.

The town of Killorglin is on a hill overlooking the River Laune. Every August the town comes alive with the Puck Fair in which a mountain goat is crowned 'King'. No one knows the origin of this custom, but it may go far back into pagan times and rituals. To the south the mountains of Macgillycuddy's Reeks rise to 3414 feet.

At the foot of Seefin Mountain is found Glenbeigh, noted for incomparable

GAP OF DUNLOE, KERRY
Right: Munster's County Kerry, in the south-west corner of Ireland, is famed for its natural beauty. Particularly worth seeing are the lakes of Killarney and the spectacular scenery along the coastal route called the 'Ring of Kerry'.

mountain scenery. A walk called the 'Glenbeigh Horseshoe' is a truly memorable experience in which one can see corries, or hollows, and glacial lakes formed during the Great Ice Age.

Just before turning south-east, the traveller comes to Cahirciveen at the base of Bentee Mountain. There are several interesting walks in and around the town itself, but perhaps the most interesting features are actually offshore. Valentia Island, joined by a bridge to the mainland and rich in tropical vegetation, offers spectacular views. And several miles out from Valentia are the magnificent Skellig Rocks, the largest of which rises some 700 feet or more. On this rock are the ruins of the most intact ancient monastic site in Europe.

Next on the tour of the Ring one comes upon Waterville, just on the edge of one of the Gaeltacht areas where Gaelic is the spoken language. On the east is Ballinskelligs Bay and on the west Lake Currane, thought by many to be the most beautiful – and dramatic – lake in Ireland. Mountains rise from its shoreline and several islands are surrounded by its waters.

One follows the coastline more closely now and passes through Caherdaniel near the hermitage of St Crohane, cut from solid rock; the Staigue Fort, a curious and well-preserved piece of Ireland's past; the little villages Castlecove and Westcove, Parknasilla and Sneem.

Finally, we come to Kenmare, not only a beautifully situated town in its

GALLARUS ORATORY
Above: This medieval chapel, for private worship, is located near the sea, in County Kerry. Its construction uses techniques similar to those used in the Bronze Age.

THE MOUNTAINS OF
MOURNE
*Overleaf: Good walking
country for nature lovers and
experienced climbers, the
Mountains of Mourne are
situated in County Down,
in Northern Ireland.*

own right, but also an ideal place from which to see much of this part of Ireland. The lace-making at the Convent of the Poor Clares is world-famous and can be viewed daily. Not far out of the town itself is a stone circle of prehistoric origin, consisting of 15 stones in a ring about 50 feet in diameter. At the centre of the circle is one large dolmen.

After completing the Ring of Kerry, the sightseer might wish to go on to Killarney. The town is interesting with its tours, markets, cultural life, and nineteenth century cathedral. But the area around it is rich in sights such as Ross Castle, now in ruins, which was significant in the Cromwellian Wars. Muckross Abbey and Muckross House, the latter surrounded by beautiful gardens, are easy to reach and there are guided tours available for both sites.

Knock

The small village of Knock is seven miles from Claremorris in County Mayo, north-east of the Tuam to Castlebar road. Set amid quiet and undramatic countryside the village has a single claim to renown, a shrine of the Blessed Virgin which attracts pilgrims from all over the world.

The tradition of the Virgin's appearance is now just over one century old. On the evening of 21 August 1879, the eve of the Octave of the Assumption, the apparition was claimed to have been seen in the parish church by several witnesses. Throughout the next four days news of the occurrence spread rapidly and almost overnight Knock became a place of pilgrimage.

Today the facilities at Knock have been expanded to receive the ever-increasing numbers of pilgrims and tourists. Visitors are received in a modern church designed with elegance and vitality, and a calendar of special services is arranged throughout the year. In 1979 celebrations of the centenary of the Virgin's appearance were crowned by the visit of His Holiness Pope John Paul II.

Accommodation at Knock is best booked in advance of a planned visit. There are many welcoming farmhouses in the surrounding countryside and information about them may be obtained through the Irish Tourist Board. Enquiries about individual or group pilgrimages can be made to the Knock Shrine Bureau, 29 South Anne Street, Dublin 2, or to Reverend Parish Priest, Knock Shrine, County Mayo.

Island Magee

The long coastal peninsula of 'Island Magee' in County Antrim stretches out its crooked arm northwards from Whitehead to form the seven mile inlet of Larne Lough. The two small jetties of Portmuck and Brown's Bay can be reached by ferry from Larne itself or by road from Whitehead. An easy bus journey from Belfast, Island Magee is famous today for its sandy coves and rocks.

In prehistoric days Island Magee was in fact a true island. More recently the Magee family, the ancient controllers of the 15-square-mile demesne, were protected on the landward side by fortifications, the last of which – Castle Chichester – is now a crumbling ruin within the boundaries of Whitehead. Documents from the reign of Elizabeth I record that the extraordinary rental of an annual supply of goshawks was exacted by the Queen in exchange for the tenure of the peninsula. Goshawks still breed on Island Magee, but the threat of captivity no longer hangs over them.

The most remarkable feature of the terrain is The Gobbins, a series of cave-riddled cliffs on the eastern shore, once the centre of Stone and Iron Age cultures. A worn walkway at the foot of the cliffs leads to a number of these caves, where burial urns, tools and jewellery have been discovered. A Neolithic tomb or 'dolmen', known locally as The Druid's Altar, confirms the habitation of the caves at an early date. Nearby the intriguing feature of The Rocking Stone – a finely balanced boulder poised on a promontory of rock – is entirely the work of nature.

Island Magee produced the last conviction for witchcraft in Ireland in 1711. A similar charge was made against a Magee woman as late as 1808, but the case was dismissed without coming to trial.

The Mountains of Mourne

The famous hills of Mourne are delightfully situated in a broad peninsula stretching south-west from the town of Newcastle in County Down. Covering a crescent-shaped area almost 15 miles long and seven miles broad, they provide a genuine challenge to experienced climbers, while the lower slopes give a variety of scenery to non-specialists who enjoy a walking holiday. No less than 11 of the peaks are over 2000 feet high.

131

The Mountains of Mourne are named after the 'Mugdahorna' a sub-division of the local MacMahon clan who left their home in County Monaghan in the twelfth century and settled in the southern part of what is now County Down. The lofty hills among which they chose to live are formed by granite thrust up at an unknown date through the older Silurian rock. Gaining in height as they reach towards the north-east the chain of hills contains over 20 peaks, many of them prefixed with the word 'Slieve', the anglicized spelling of the Irish 'sliabh', a mountain. Sliabh Donard, 2796 feet high, is the highest mountain in Ulster.

The terrain is rough and the glens of the many streams flowing towards the sea are often strewn with boulders and broken by ridges of peat. The Bann, the longest and best-known of the rivers which rise in the Mourne Mountains, flows north and its headwaters run close to the Spegla Pass, the single road which traverses the range.

The vistas are magnificent from anywhere. Most notable is the view at the top of Slieve Donard from where the Donegal Hills, the Wicklow Mountains, the Isle of Man and the Scottish coast are all distinctly visible on a clear day. On the summit an ancient cairn marks the burial place of the bardic hero

Slainge after whom the peak was originally named. Celtic annals of the region record Slainge's death in 'anno mundi 2533', that is 2533 years after the creation of the world.

Deep in the hills lies the romantically named Silent Valley. From here a reservoir provides 20,000,000 gallons of water each day to Belfast.

Powerscourt Waterfall

Powerscourt Waterfall, the longest river drop in Ireland, is part of the extensive Powerscourt demesne close to the village of Enniskerry about three miles west of Bray in County Wicklow. Both the wooded village and the gardens of the house with their views over the Dargle Valley are among the most beautiful in Ireland.

Powerscourt Waterfall is situated four miles upstream from Powerscourt House beyond the extensive deer park. It is an enchanting freak of nature: a tremulous shower of brilliant water in summer, in winter and after rains it becomes an impressive torrent, the stream hurtling at an acute angle across a 400 foot cliff and crashing to the river bed below. The rarest and most beautiful sight of all is after severe frost when the watercourse freezes and icy tendrils hang from the face of the rocks.

ISLAND MAGEE
Above: The Rocking Stone, a feature of this long peninsula, which in prehistoric times was a true island. Relics of Stone and Iron Age cultures have been found in caves along its shores.

POWERSCOURT WATERFALL
Right: This 400-foot waterfall is one of the attractions of the Powerscourt estate, which also includes an imposing eighteenth century house and beautiful gardens offering a view of the Wicklow Mountains.

It is a strange chance that the best of landscape gardening and the best of natural beauty should meet in this one place. In 1821 an intriguing attempt was made to 'landscape' the waterfall itself for the visit of George IV to Powerscourt. In order that the Dargle might show itself to the royal visitor with particular radiance a dam was erected above the falls to store up an extra head of water for the King's arrival.

George, however, was lured by the more tangible pleasures of a long dinner and decided not to come. When this news reached the workmen at the falls they opened the dam, whereupon the Dargle leaped forward with such vigour that it swept away the bridge from which the King was to have watched the spectacle.

Powerscourt Waterfall can be visited throughout the year between 10.30 a.m. and 8.00 p.m.

Scotland

Loch Trool in SW Scotland (Dumfries and Galloway). Lochs (lakes) are enduring features of Scotland's geography especially in the Highlands.

Abbotsford, Home of Sir Walter Scott

Abbotsford today is both museum and residence, continuing to reflect the sense of history which inspired Sir Walter Scott's work.

In 1811 Scott paid 4000 guineas for a farm near Ashiestiel. The farmhouse was pulled down in 1822 and the architect William Atkinson, with much advice from Scott and his friends, began the building of the great Gothic baronial hall, Abbotsford.

Scott failed in a business venture and died at Abbotsford, as he predicted, 'in harness', driving himself to repay his company's debts. Yet the mansion conveys a sense of affluence throughout, and the wealth of the furnishings and relics it contains are as much of historical as of intrinsic value.

The rich oak panelling in the Entrance Hall is from the Auld Kirk of Dunfermline. Here a wide diversity of objects is displayed, including two highland back swords from the field of Culloden, the keys of the old Tolbooth prison, and the skull and horns of an extinct breed of Scottish cattle.

In the Study, Scott's handsome desk and worn, comfortable chair occupy the centre of a room lined with books. A door opens on to the Library, which has an elaborately carved wood ceiling and which shares with the study Scott's collection of 9000 volumes.

Next door is the Drawing Room where the family portraits hang, including a large painting of Scott and his greyhound Percy by Sir Henry Raeburn. The fine Portuguese roll-top desk and chairs were a gift from George IV, and in a wall case is a silver urn presented by Lord Byron. The many gifts and presentations displayed throughout give some indication of Scott's stature, particularly as a Scotsman who worked hard to promote his country's heritage.

In the Armoury a contemporary portrait of James IV holding a Tudor rose makes a peaceful statement amid a fine display of dirks, daggers and firearms which include Scott's own blunderbuss. The ante-room to the Armoury holds paintings and miniatures, including portraits of Scott's ancestors and his household, and Landseer's painting of Ginger, one of the writer's dogs. Other family portraits hang in the Dining Room, where the table is set with a Coalport dinner service. Here in 1832, at the age of 61, Scott died. Abbotsford is occupied by his descendants to this day.

ABBOTSFORD
Sir Walter Scott's desk, where he wrote many of his novels, can be seen at his home, Abbotsford, near Melrose. The house, erected in the 1820s, is a turreted and gabled structure, as romantic as Scott's own writing. Nostalgia for the Middle Ages may have inspired its architecture, but it was one of the first country houses in Britain to be lit by gaslight.

Braemar

Braemar Castle, situated about 40 miles west of Aberdeen, was built in 1628 by the second Earl of Mar who intended it to be used mainly as a hunting lodge. However, with its commanding position high above the River Dee, the castle also presented a warning to the rival Farquharson family that the Mars were well able to defend their territory.

In 1688, the then Earl of Mar declared for William of Orange and the castle was turned into a garrison for Government troops. A year later the Farquharsons, Jacobite supporters, attacked Braemar and with the Mars routed set fire to the castle. It was to languish as a burnt-out shell until 1748 when the architect John Adam was commissioned to restore the castle by the Hanoverian Government. Upon completion, the Government leased it from the Farquharsons – by then its owners – and quartered troops there until the expiration of the 99-year lease. Once again it became the Farquharsons' family home and residence.

The fact that Braemar was always potentially more than a mere hunting lodge can be seen in its massive iron gateway or *yett* and the deep pit prisons characteristic of Scotland's old tower houses. Other points of interest are the star-shaped defensive wall, the barrel-vaulted ceilings, the round central tower and a spiral staircase leading to the principal rooms. The walls of the living quarters still show traces of graffiti carved by its soldier occupants.

The nearby village of Braemar is renowned for the Royal Highland Gathering in early September, which follows the Highland Games held at Balater in mid-August and Aboyne at the beginning of September. These games are a fairly modern tradition on a grand scale, a development of the small impromptu Games held in 1850 for Queen Victoria.

Culzean Castle and Country Park

Culzean Castle is the showpiece of the Ayrshire coast. Once a typical Scottish fort, the castle was transformed by Robert Adam in about 1777 and is now a vast, romantic castellated mansion set amid semi-tropical formal gardens. Mansion and gardens face the hills of Arran across a westering sea; beneath the cliff on which they stand are Culzean Coves, used as hiding places in the Civil wars, where Burns' hobgoblins gather at

Halloween, the evening of 31 October.

Robert Adam integrated the original simple medieval structure into a building which matched Gothic mass with classic symmetry. He created classical interiors to rival the final culmination, an oval staircase of exquisite elegance. In each room are fireplaces, mirrors, ceilings, incorporated by Adams to his own design. Perhaps the finest room is the Round Drawing Room, beautifully furnished, with a circular carpet specially woven in the neighbouring town of Maybole, and windows overlooking the shore 200 feet below. The National Trust for Scotland maintains the building and its 565 acres of garden and park, and has restored much of the Castle's interior, retrieving original plasterwork mouldings from a workshop.

Adam also designed the castle's home farm complex, and in 1969 these stylish, functional buildings were restored and established as a centre for the country park. NTS park rangers maintain the land and they arrange guided walks for those who wish to learn about the nature of the countryside. These activities are backed up, at the centre, with filing lectures and displays.

The wild cliffs, shore and woodland of the country park are matched in beauty by Culzean's formal gardens which include the palmed fountain court, a walled garden of 1783, an aviary and swan pond and successive flowerings of snowdrops, camellias, hydrangeas and bamboo, among many indigenous and exotic plants, throughout the year.

Dryburgh Abbey

The ruined abbey stands surrounded by trees on a grassy peninsula, around which swirl the waters of the Tweed. One of the four great Border abbeys, Dryburgh was founded by Hugh de Morville for the Premonstration canons in about 1152. It was twice reduced by the English in the thirteenth century and twice in the sixteenth, and thereafter was allowed to decay. Little is left of the church apart from a magnificent shell, but the monastery buildings remain among the most characteristic and the most complete of any in Scotland. They give an intriguing account of the monks' way of life in the late twelfth and thirteenth centuries.

From the ruined nave of the church the cloister is entered by a deeply recessed semicircular Norman Arch, the capitals decorated in Early English leaf ornament, an example of the Transi-

tional style of architecture characteristic of the abbey buildings. There are three entrances in the east wall of the cloister. The first leads to the Vestry, later converted into St Modan's Chapel (named after an abbot of an earlier, sixth century monastery) which is also entered from the south transept of the church. The second entrance opens on to the Parlour, where the monks were allowed to meet outsiders; and the third enters the Chapter House. Here the barrel-vaulted roof and the stone bench, which is arcaded at the east end where the abbot sat, are all intact. Openings to either side of the entrance allowed lay brothers to listen as the monks read and discussed their Rule. A stair leads to the Dormitory, and an entrance south opens on to the Calefactory where the monks assembled around a vast fireplace, still preserved.

Farthest south, separated by a passage, is the Novices' Day Room and to the east of the Calefactory, flanking the south wall of the cloister, is the Refectory. A great rose window remains.

In the north transept aisle of the church are the burial places of Sir Walter Scott, whose ancestors owned the abbey lands for a while, and of Earl Haig, and their families. Earl Haig's tomb is often strewn with Flanders poppies. An ancient juniper tree, supported by props, grows outside the Chapter House, and a yew tree growing near the boundary wall is said to be as old as the abbey.

Edinburgh Castle

The castle dominates Edinburgh, standing starkly on a rock in the heart of the city, occupying its loftiest and most ancient site. Records of the castle as a royal residence date back to its occupation by Malcolm II of Scotland in 1004. Later in the eleventh century the Anglo-Saxon Princess Margaret, fugitive from the Normans, came here as wife of the Celtic king, Malcolm III.

The gentle but determined Margaret was active in gathering the Celtic Christian groups together under the universal Church of Rome. In 1076 she began the tiny chapel of rough stone which stands in the Citadel at the summit of Castle Rock today. St Margaret's Chapel is thought to be the earliest Roman Catholic building in Scotland and its unique position in Scottish history has prevented its destruction on occasions when all else on Castle Rock and in the Old Town has been razed to the ground. Its simple interior, which

DRYBURGH ABBEY
Overleaf: The ruins of this medieval abbey contain the graves of Sir Walter Scott and Field Marshal Haig.

BRAEMAR CASTLE
Built originally in 1628, Braemar, in Aberdeenshire, was captured by Jacobite supporters in 1689 but occupied by the Hanoverian government forces after the final defeat of the Stuart cause in 1746. Now it is a private residence.

seats a congregation of 26, is lit by Victorian windows depicting Celtic saints, St Margaret, and the thirteenth century patriot, William Wallace.

Steep steps lead up from the Portcullis gate and the State Prison, scene of past suffering, to the chapel which overlooks Edinburgh, the sea, and the distant shores of Fife. Also overlooking this scene is Mons Meg, 'the lass wi' the iron mou', a replica of a 12-foot, five-ton cannon that could fire a five-hundred-weight blast at a range of a mile and a half.

The apex of Castle Rock, near the chapel, is now occupied by the Scottish National War Memorial, which forms the northern side of Palace Yard. The Memorial was built in 1927 to commemorate the fallen of the 1914–18 'war to end all wars'. In the Hall of Honour the names of the dead are enshrined in a beautiful casket presented by King George V and Queen Mary. The casket is set into the bare rock projecting through the floor of this noble building, which now also contains the Roll of Honour for World War II.

The Memorial faces the sixteenth century Banqueting Hall across Palace Yard. Here, it is thought, early Scottish parliaments met. Now it displays a fine collection of Scottish armoury, and royal banquets are sometimes held under its oaken hammerbeam roof. Still grand affairs, they happily lack the savage intrigue of past banquets, like the notorious Black Dinner of 1440 when a black bull's head was placed upon the table. After the feast, given in honour of the young Earl of Douglas and his brother, King James II's henchmen executed their unsuspecting guests.

Along the east of the quadrangle are the Royal Apartments, and here in 1503 James IV brought his bride, Princess Margaret Tudor, sister of Henry VIII. Here too, in a small cramped room, Mary Queen of Scots gave birth to the infant James VI of Scotland, later to become James I of England thus uniting the Scottish and English crowns. Legend has it that, to keep the baby out of danger, he had to be lowered in a basket down the precipitous face of Castle Rock from the mean east window.

CULZEAN CASTLE
Above: Designed by Robert Adam, Culzean is unusual in being neo-gothic in style, rather than neo-classical like most of his work, though the interior contains some typically fine plasterwork. Shown here: the Music Room.

EDINBURGH CASTLE
Right: Today, as for many centuries, Edinburgh Castle dominates the city, overlooking both the Old Town and the New. From the eleventh century to the sixteenth it was used as a residence by Scottish kings and queens.

144

Close by, in the vaulted Crown Room, the Scottish Crown Jewels are displayed. The regalia includes the crown worn by Robert Bruce, and the golden collar of the Order of the Garter conferred on James VI by Elizabeth I of England, whom he was to succeed; and poignant reminders of independent Scotland's Roman Catholic kings and queens of whom the first was the saintly Margaret, and the last, the ill-starred Mary, Queen of Scots.

Charlotte Square and Princes Street

Edinburgh's New Town, one of the most noble and the most complete survivals of Georgian town planning, ranks high among its counterparts of this period, not only in Britain, but in all of Europe. It occupies the site of Nor' Loch which once lay north of the ridge on which Old Edinburgh stands. In the era of security following union with England, the civic authorities seized the unique opportunity of developing this neglected terrain; they resisted ad hoc building and initiated the design of this spacious and dignified rectangular layout of boulevards and squares which, two centuries later, is still known as New Town.

In 1767, the first foundation stone was laid by Scheme's Architect, James Craig, for a house which was to be part of the central parade, George Street. In 1791, Robert Adam designed Charlotte Square, the western culmination of George Street, and the masterpiece of the New Town.

On the west side of the square is the massive St George's Church, now used by the Scottish Records Office, which was built after Adam's death. Its green dome, emulating London's St Paul's, closes the vista along George Street. The perfectly preserved north side, thought to rank among the finest street façades in Europe, is best seen from across the grassed, wooded gardens in the centre of the square. The houses Nos 5, 6 and 7, once the property of the Marquess of Bute, now belong to the National Trust. Bute House, No 6, is the official residence of the Secretary of State for Scotland; No 5 houses the headquarters of the National Trust, and No 7, open to the public, is restored as a typical Georgian residence. This harmonious group forms the centrepiece of Charlotte Square, which has been described by Sir Basil Spence as 'civic architecture at its best, created by a master'.

Queen Street and Princes Street contain the northern and southern margins of 'these draughty parallelograms' as the broad straight streets of the New Town have been called; the tenements and wynds of the Old Town may well have provided better protection against Edinburgh's merciless east wind. Princes Street, like Queen Street, is occupied by buildings along only one side. Now much altered, it is a fashionable centre of mixed architecture, and Edinburgh's most noted promenade. But the view Craig devised of Old Town's jumbled skyline and of Edinburgh Castle, dramatic by daylight and spectacular when floodlit, remains uninterrupted, with a foreground of gardens laid out along the foot of the slopes bordering Princes Street, full of statues and flowers.

Princes Street Gardens are divided by the Mound, which leads to the Royal Mill. Where the Mound begins stands the Floral Clock, a huge ornamental timepiece. Opposite it is the Royal Scottish Academy, and next door, the National Gallery of Scotland. The RSA presents predominantly Scottish work by living artists, while the National Gallery contains a fine collection of European paintings from the fourteenth to the early twentieth century including works by Tiepolo, Goya, and El Greco; among the paintings of seventeenth century masters is Rembrandt's *A Woman in Bed*. French Impressionist paintings are represented, and of the English painters Gainsborough, Turner and Constable are shown. There is an interesting section of Scottish artists, among them Raeburn and Ramsey (who was also active as a poet and writer). Both Raeburn and Ramsey lived and worked in Edinburgh.

At the far end of Princes Street, facing North Bridge, another Robert Adam masterpiece, Register House, makes a fitting repository for the Scottish National Archives. Lawyers and researchers consult modern legal records under an Adam ceiling in the central dome. Records in the Historical Search Room, which include letters from Mary, Queen of Scots, date from a charter to the Abbey of Melrose in 1137 to the present day.

Dominating this end of Princes Street from the gardens by Waverley Street is the stirring memorial to Sir Walter Scott, who was also a native of Edinburgh. Those who climb to the platform beneath the monument's Gothic spire, 200 feet high, can appreciate Craig's concept of the gardens, terraces, churches,

and squares as one integrated design.

The formal grandeur of Queen Street Gardens, Royal Circus, the gracious Heriot Row, the central Great King Street, Fettes Rown and Drummond Place, further away from the heart of Edinburgh have remained more nearly unaltered and retained their Georgian grace.

Royal Mile

Scotland's history as an independent nation is rooted in the Royal Mile. For centuries all of Edinburgh was crowded along this rocky ridge descending steeply east from Castle Rock, with the separate burgh of Canongate, continuing west to Holyrood Abbey and the palace. Development of low-lying land to the north was impeded by Nor' Loch, and any settlement to the south would have weakened the town's defences against English raids. So evolved some of the earliest high-rise living in Europe and until union with England in 1707 the capital of Scotland comprised the huddled, picturesque strip which came to be known as the Royal Mile.

From about the fifteenth century, tall wooden dwellings, known as 'lands', accommodating several families (commoners occupying the lower storeys, the nobility the top floors), clung to either side of the ridge. Stairways and wynds or passages led steeply down to other dwellings, closes and courts. The district was companionable, insalubrious and prone to fire.

After the 'rough wooing' of Henry

VIII had wiped out almost the whole of Edinburgh and the Abbey in 1544, the Royal Mile was rebuilt in stone and the fire risk reduced.

However, problems of imposing any kind of sewer system in this rocky terrain remained unsolved, and the late night practice of hurling household waste from the windows with a cry of 'Gardy loo!' (from the French 'Gardez l'eau!') continued to excite comment from visitors like Dr Johnson, whose murmured verdict in 1773 on the sights of Edinburgh to his companion Boswell was, 'I smell you in the dark'.

Today, with very few exceptions, the earliest buildings date from the sixteenth and seventeenth centuries. Many have been restored or reconstructed under the Royal Mile Development Plan and much of Edinburgh's Old Town is preserved.

One Victorian diversion is a camera obscura, which projects on to a white concave tabletop an image of the Old Town, the New Town and modern Edinburgh.

Castle Hill descends to Lawnmarket, the medieval site of a land market where country produce was sold, and here one of the finest surviving sixteenth century dwellings may be seen. Owned by the National Trust, Gladstone's Land has an arcade, ground-floor crow-stepped gables and outside stairway, equalled by an interior of period furnishings and ceilings painted with fruit and flowers. The house was started in the 1550s and was acquired in 1617 by the Edinburgh merchant Thomas Gladstane, who added the piazza, the last of its kind to survive in Edinburgh. Close by is Lady Stair's house built in 1622, characteristically tall, narrow and sturdily ornate with balconies and a dome. Lady Stair was a great society lady. Her house is now a museum devoted to Robert Burns, Sir Walter Scott and Robert Louis Stevenson.

The heart of Edinburgh's Old Town in High Street, below Lawnmarket, is gathered around St Giles' Cathedral. Here John Knox, spearhead of the Scottish Reformation, preached his first sermon in 1559; here, the legendary episode nearly one century later, when Jenny Geddes hurled a stool at Dean Hannay's head, marking the beginning of the Church of Scotland's stance against Charles I's command to replace John Knox's Bible with the Anglican Liturgy. The cathedral's official title, the High Kirk of St Giles, resulted from that movement. There has been a church on this site from the ninth century, but the present building is uncompromisingly Victorian Gothic, except for a magnificent fifteenth century tower in the form of an imperial crown. The Thistle Chapel, meeting place of the venerable Knights of the Thistle, the highest order of Scottish chivalry, is a beautiful example of early twentieth century Gothic architecture.

A heart-shaped design in parti-coloured cobbles at St Giles's west door marks the site of the Tolbooth Prison, the scene of the Porteous Riots of 1726. Near here, hard by the walls of the church, a medieval bazaar of Luckenbooths and Krames – 'locked booths' and stalls – flourished until the Tolbooth was demolished in 1817. The Victorian replica of the original Mercat Cross, incorporating its 'lang stane' or shaft, stands at the east end of St Giles. In the twelfth century, this stone cross was a venue for trading, proclamations, public rejoicing and executions. Royal proclamations are still read here by the Lord Lyon King of Arms.

To the south of the church is the classic façade of Parliament House where from 1639 until union with England in 1707 the Scottish supreme courts sat. Under the lofty timbers of the hammerbeam roof of Parliament Hall, Scottish advocates, gowned and wigged, are to be seen in discussion with clients and colleagues in a setting of statues and portraits; and the great south window depicts James V's inauguration of the Court of Session in 1532.

At the far end of High Street, near the site of Netherbow, the gate which marked the beginning of the ecclesiastical burgh of the Canongate, is John Knox's House. It was built about 1490 and its remarkable timber galleries are the only remaining examples from this period. The painted ceilings in the Oak Room, dating from 1600, are also very fine. Despite the fact that John Knox's residence during 1561–72 is debatable, the house contains many of Knox's possessions, his bed-closet, and the study where it is said he worked until a fortnight before his death in 1572.

The former occupant of Knox's House was James Mossman, whose intials and those of his wife are carved on a wood panel. Mossman was goldsmith to Mary, Queen of Scots, in whose cause he died. Another of his inscriptions in large Roman letters admonishes 'Lufe God abufe al, and thi nichbour as thi-self'.

Before leaving High Street it is worth

descending the narrow, steep stairways and wynds to the old closes and courts, among them Roxborough Close. The Old Town's history is present in their names and their stones. Sudden panoramas of modern Edinburgh are glimpsed between the lofty lands.

The Canongate covers one-third of the Royal Mile, leading from High Street to Holyroodhouse and the Abbey ruins. The area round the gait or road of the Augustinian monks, who occupied the Abbey until the twelfth century, was founded as a separate burgh by royal charter in 1143. So it remained until absorbed in the nineteenth century. After the union it ceased to be a fashionable residence for the nobility and by the nineteenth century, it had become a slum; but many notable residences remain, and recently much has been restored and replaced.

A building that has survived without extensive restoration is the Canongate Tolbooth built in the French style with conical turrets, and with a large Victorian clock now jutting over the street. Once Canongate's Courthouse and Council Rooms, it is an interesting and very beautiful example of Scottish sixteenth century municipal architecture. The seventeenth century Canongate Church nearby has been beautifully restored.

Across the street, is Huntly House. Dating in part from the fifteenth century, this splendid, well-restored mansion was known as the 'Speaking House', since the builder, guilty perhaps at erecting such a substantial dwelling on a site where land was scarce, had installed a series of Latin inscriptions: one read, 'Today I am a happy man; tomorrow it may be your turn'. The City Museum, occupying the entrance hall and some eighteen rooms, displays Edinburgh glass, Scottish pottery, and many documents and maps illustrating local history.

An impressive example of Canongate reconstruction is White Horse Close, once a terminus for the London Coach. The White Horse Inn, said to be named after Mary, Queen of Scots' white palfrey, featured in Sir Walter Scott's novel *Waverley* as a meeting place for Bonny Prince Charlie's army in 1745. Earlier, tradition makes it the meeting place for Scots nobles on their way to parley with Charles I at Berwick in 1639 – unsuccessfully, as it turned out. The Inn has been converted into residences and the Close, retaining all its seventeenth century dwellings, furnishes twentieth century comforts behind the

crow-stepped gables, red pantiled roofs, dormer windows and stone stairways of another age.

The Royal Mile ends at the entrance to Holyroodhouse. The letter S set at intervals into the ground marks the space by the watergate that was 'in sanctuary' until 1888. So the old gait of the monks witnessed many an ignominious chase between bailiff and debtor, who could not be arrested on Abbey ground – long after the abbey had been sacked, deserted and ruined.

Fort William and Ben Nevis

At the south-western extreme of the Great Glen is Fort William, a major centre for touring the West Highlands and the Western Isles. In 1654 Cromwell built the original Fort of earth and wattle near Inverlochy Castle, a traditionally strategic position from which to control the West Highlands. In 1690 William III reconstructed it of stone, and in the uprising of 1745 it was unsuccessfully besieged by the Jacobites. One hundred and fifty years later, the fort was levelled to make way for the railway.

The town, standing on a principal road and rail route and in the centre of the important industrial area of the western seaboard, supports its own distilleries and industrial plants. Sited on the shore of Loch Linnhe, at the foot of the cloud-capped Ben Nevis, Fort William is within reach of some of Scotland's most inspiring and historic scenery.

This hillside town, is predominantly Victorian; the imposing St Andrew's Episcopal Church dominates the main street.

In Cameron Square, the West Highlands Museum holds the best collection of local historical exhibits on the west coast. Among the Jacobite relics is a secret portrait of Bonnie Prince Charlie which appears only when reflected in a curved and polished surface.

The gates of the original Fort now form the entrance to the Craig Burial Ground at the north of the town. Near here is the Bridge of Nevis which leads past Cow Hill to Ben Nevis, at 4406 feet the highest mountain in Britain. The popular ascent starts at Achintee Farm in the beautiful Glen Nevis, and provides walkers with some stiff scrambling over rough, rocky terrain. The path leads beneath 2000-foot cliffs, eroded into ridges and towers, each individually named.

BEN NEVIS
Overleaf: The highest mountain in Britain (4406 feet), Ben Nevis stands at the edge of Fort William.

JOHN KNOX'S HOUSE, EDINBURGH
The Calvinist preacher and implacable foe of Mary, Queen of Scots is said to have lived here between 1561 and 1572. It contains a fine painted ceiling and many of Knox's belongings.

HERMITAGE CASTLE
Overleaf: Situated in the Border country, Hermitage Castle was frequently involved in the savage wars between the Scots and English during the Middle Ages. At one time it belonged to the Earl of Bothwell, third husband of Mary, Queen of Scots.

BEN NEVIS
Left: Snow lies on the mountain all year while its summit was once home for a small hotel and weather observatory.

PALACE OF HOLYROODHOUSE
Right: Most closely associated with Mary, Queen of Scots, whose secretary Rizzio was murdered in one of its rooms, Holyroodhouse was begun in the early sixteenth century. It is still a royal palace and is used by the Queen when she visits the Scottish capital.

The summit is rounded, not peaked, scattered with boulders and subject to highly unpredictable weather. It is well known that even in summer boots should be worn and warm clothing carried, for Ben Nevis can be treacherous.

Clear weather, however, reveals an exhilarating spectacle of peaks and lochs spreading as far as the eye can see. South-west across the sea is the island of Mull, north-west is Skye, and reaching northward between mountains to the far shore is the Great Glen.

Hermitage Castle

The huge and forbidding bulk of Hermitage Castle, flanked by ancient grassed ramparts, broods over marshy moorland grazed by sheep. Just south of the main façade, Hermitage Water flows placidly past. For centuries castle, ramparts, marsh and river formed the stronghold which held the stategic key to the length of the Border's Liddesdale Valley. Today the Border region is noted for its production of woven and knitted goods; the castle, obdurate but not unhandsome, speaks of the Border's savage past. Some of the cruellest and most malicious acts of those times were perpetrated in and around this vitally important fortress, which changed hands endlessly from the time of the Scottish Wars of Independence during the thirteenth and fourteenth centuries until 1603, when the crowns of Scotland and England were joined.

The castle's fifteenth century exterior, built by the Douglasses, was extensively restored last century, and it belies the ruinous state of the interior. Dwarfed by the massive towers of the south façade, an arched doorway opens

vrote 'Alice in Wonderland'

75 cents

The researchers spent thousands of hours deciphering "Alice."

Queen Victoria kept extensive diaries throughout her life. Some were published and many were burned after her death.

Under the theory proposed by the Continental Historical Society, the queen wanted to "have her cake and eat it." She resented very much her childhood and wanted to "get it off her chest." But, because she still was reigning,

she felt she had to do it in a secret way.

Not only has the society come up with an interpretation for every incident and allusion in the story, but it has conducted a computer study that is said to prove "Alice" and "Looking Glass" are similar (they say identical) to Queen Victoria's known writings and unlike anything Dodgson had written.

For example, in her childhood diaries the

ur is Prince Albert, the she loved so dearly.

president of the Continental and chief editor of its nization as an "ad hoc have been speculating of "Alice" since 1973 letters in The London les Dodgson was not

See ALICE, back of section.

From Page 1A

Alice

The by allo "Alice", Glass," illustrat hidden Dodg The res say Do queen

In include college therapi sor of curator Big Sur

The torical Queen drug been recen Nu was her h of he expla had descr In actua area. "sun said port by u the f princ on to the oldest surviving part, a long narrow courtyard, typical of British manor houses of the fourteenth century. At the north end a rounded entrance gives on to a spiral staircase leading as far as first-floor level. Here doors to left and right would have led to passages and thence on the west side, it is thought, to the great hall; on the east side to the lord of the castle's private apartments. It would have been in these chambers that in 1566 Mary Queen of Scots visited her wounded Bothwell, between riding the 25 miles from Jedburgh and back the same day. The episode damaged Mary's reputation, and brought on a fever that threatened her life.

On the ground floor the north and south towers of the east flank date from about 1400. In the south-east tower, besides interesting defensive features, is a well which still supplies good water. The north-east tower, situated under what was a first-floor prison, is an airless and lightless pit, once entered from a trap above. It is similar to the earlier dungeon in which the Knight of Liddesdale Sir William Douglas, in 1342, allowed Sir Alexander Ramsay to starve to death. This was by no means the worst deed done at Hermitage Castle, and the part-fact, part-supernatural tales of misdeeds add to the building's aura of eerie gloom.

In the basement of the south-west tower are the pleasantly domestic remains of the kitchen.

Holyrood Abbey and Palace

Holyroodhouse Palace, looking much like a French château, backed by the ancient, skeletal Abbey ruins, contains the eastern limit of Edinburgh's Old Town and of the Royal Mile. Despite successive devastation by the English, Abbey and palace were the principal seat of the Scottish monarchy through the turbulent centuries leading to the Union of Crowns.

The ruins of Holyrood (Holy Cross) Abbey date from 1128, when a Franciscan house was founded here by David I, who built the chapel on Castle Rock. Over the centuries it was well endowed and gradually became a royal residence. Holyroodhouse was begun in 1502 as a home for James IV's bride Margaret Tudor, and the royal residency moved away from the Abbey. The palace was sacked with the rest of Edinburgh by Henry VIII in 1544 and 1547, and in 1650 it was burned by Cromwell's men; in 1671 it was rebuilt

by Charles II in the French style, and so it remains. Facing west along the Royal Mile, a noble entrance of Doric columns is flanked north and south by twin towers; the north one survives from James IV's original palace.

Holyroodhouse Palace is the official residence of the Queen when she is in Edinburgh. The State Apartments, on the south and east of the quadrangle, are noted for their panelling and ceilings, their French and Flemish tapestries and eighteenth century furniture, which was installed by Queen Victoria. On the north side, the Picture Gallery is hung with portraits (of dubious validity) of all the Scottish kings, painted in the 1680s by James de Witt. In this Gallery, which Sir Walter Scott described as a 'long, low and ill-proportioned' room, the Young Pretender Charles Edward held levees during his brief triumph in 1745. From here the Historical Apartments, situated in the original tower, are entered. This is where Mary, Queen of Scots, lived during the six years of her troubled reign.

On the first floor are the apartments of Mary's husband Lord Darnley, his bedroom and dressing room, hung with portraits and tapestries. A staircase from the audience chamber leads up to the Queen's apartments; a private staircase, closed to the public, also gave access to the Queen's rooms.

Behind the wall hangings of the Queen's dressing room, in the east turret, concealed stairways and entrances lead to the supper room in the east turret. One account has it that here, in 1566, a group of dissident nobles, among them the Queen's weak and jealous husband, dragged her secretary, David Rizzio, from the presence of the pregnant Queen and her companions, and murdered him at the head of the main staircase. A brass tablet marks the alleged scene of the crime.

Near the staircase is the audience chamber where, after her arrival from France in 1560, the young Queen received her vehement adversary John Knox. On the panelled ceiling of the chamber and of the Queen's bedroom are emblems and intials of Scottish sovereigns, and the bedroom walls are hung with tapestries depicting the Fall of Phaeton. Some personal possessions, a mirror, embroidery worked by the Queen, and the bed claimed to be hers, are displayed. These are poignant reminders of the early years of Mary's occupation, when she indulged in needlework, music and dancing, golf, hunting

INVERARAY CASTLE
Overleaf: Built between 1743 and 1782, Inveraray is an early example of the neo-gothic style, then just beginning to become popular. It is the home of the Duke of Argyll and the headquarters of Clan Campbell.
Right: The Tapestry Drawing Room at Inveraray before the fire, in 1975, that destroyed much of the castle's interior.

and archery. But it is the events of the last two years of her reign, the murders, the failure of her marriage to Darnley, and her association and subsequent marriage with the Earl of Bothwell for which her time at Holyroodhouse is recalled.

The palace and the skeletal ruin of the twelfth century Abbey adjoin Holyrood Park, an untamed tract of springy turf from which thrust the strange basaltic formation of Samson's Ribs, the red sandstone Salisbury Crags and the hill known as Arthur's Seat, over 800 feet above the city.

Inveraray Castle

The River Aray, bound for Loch Fyne, flows through the rolling parkland of Inveraray Castle. White towers, arched windows and delicately-proportioned battlements set amid grass, water and trees make this one of the most imposing sights in Scotland. Built in the French château style popular at the time, the conical spines were added to the towers in 1877, after a fire had destroyed the top of the building. Just beyond this baronial seat, and part of the same eighteenth century scheme, are the stylish white

houses and 'lands' of Inveraray, a small town spread along the banks of Loch Fyne. The 'lands' are tall buildings similar to those in Edinburgh, and they now belong to the Department of the Environment. Their interiors have been finely restored.

Castle and town date from about 1756. They were planned to replace a fifteenth century castle and the remains of a medieval village that had been burned in 1645 by the Marquess of Montrose, an old enemy of the Argylls who were chiefs of the Clan Campbell. Inveraray was the capital of the Argylls. William Adam was Clerk of Works at the beginning of the scheme and his son, John, brother of the famous Robert Adam, completed the castle's interior for the fifth Duke of Argyll in 1782. He also designed the impressive bridge carrying the road between castle and loch.

Visitors taken with the charm of the castle's approach will find the same fairytale quality inside. The Georgian proportions and Adam fireplaces, the elaborate but fine-wrought ceilings, the Beauvais tapestries and Italian murals, form a rich setting for the exquisite furnishing and family treasures which grace each room. A disastrous fire in 1975

devastated many paintings in the castle's upper storeys, but many fine paintings remain, including family portraits by Gainsborough, Raeburn, Ramsay and Hoppner.

A splendid array of ancient Scottish armoury is displayed in the Central Hall, which dates from 1877. Among other relics to be seen at the castle are the cap worn by the eighth Earl, the first Marquess of Argyll, when he was beheaded in 1661 for his support of Cromwell; and the dirk handle and sporran of the bandit Rob Roy who lived in Glen Shira, at the Falls of Aray.

Loch Lomond

Britain's biggest and most beautiful inland water Loch Lomond, 24 miles long and of irregular width, is only four miles from the sea. At Balloch, the loch's southernmost point, the waters pour via the River Leven into the Clyde. Loch Lomond's greatest width is five miles across, and here the southern shores roll away to green hills, the banks thick with beech, oak, larch, chestnut and birch. Wooded islands cluster between the banks, and in the season the water is specked with pleasure craft.

At Rowardennan and Inverbeg on the east and west banks, the loch narrows and thrusts a long arm north past Ben Lomond into mountainous country. Surrounding heights exceed 3000 feet, while the waters deepen to 630 feet. Here the shores seem more remote; but the wild slopes echo with battle cries of rival clans, Macgregor and Macfarlane, cattle-reivers and brigands who occupied the east and west shores. Two centuries hence, natives of Loch Lomond still refer to the moon as 'Macfarlane's Lantern'.

A scenically breathtaking but seasonally crowded major road now twists along the western shore from Balloch to Ardlui, deep in mountains at the loch's northern extreme. A quieter B road follows the east bank from Balmaha northward to Rowardennan, the centre for ascents of Ben Lomond whose grassy summit, 3129 feet, gently dominates all parts of the loch. A shore path which penetrates deep into the mountains passes Inversnaid, just over three miles from Rob Roy's Cave. This beautiful village is the northernmost call of the *Maid of the Loch*, a popular paddle steamer which tours from Balloch, calling at Balmaha, Rowardennan and Tarbet before turning southward at Inversnaid. Most of these small resorts have facilities for watersports; Balloch is

famous for its bear garden. Loch Lomond in fact abounds in wildlife, and swimmers' reports of fearful encounters with giant eels in the remote deeper waters may well afford an explanation for the Loch Ness mystery.

The numerous islands in the southern waters have their history and special characteristics. Five islands today form a nature reserve noted for its wintering wildfowl, among them great northern divers, whooper swan, Slavonian and crested grebe. A ruined castle on Inchmurrin belonged to the Earls of Lennox, and the island is thought to be the site of a sixth century monastery founded by St Mirren. Inchlonaig was planted with yew trees by Robert the Bruce to provide bows for his archers.

Luss, a pretty village on the west bank facing Inchlonaig, was built by the Colquhoun family. This sole surviving local clan, whose eighteenth century mansion is open to the public, has done much to preserve the 'bonny banks and braes' of Loch Lomond.

Loch Ness

Famous for its monster, Loch Ness lies amid wild mountain scenery along one third of the deep geological fault, the Great Glen. This schism which effectively separates the Highlands from the rest of Scotland runs in a north-easterly direction from Fort William at the head of Loch Linnhe to Inverness on the Moray Firth. In the nineteenth century, the Caledonian Canal was built, linking the long, narrow lochs along the fault, from sea to sea.

Loch Ness is $22\frac{1}{2}$ miles long, never more than two miles wide, at points deeper than 700 feet and bordered by peaks reaching 2000 to 3000 feet. There is a mountain road running along the east side and a highway along the western shore from Fort Augustus to Inverness. Half-way, the highway enters the green and fertile Glen Urquhart where, on a promontory, the ruin of a fourteenth century castle broods over waters reaching a depth of 750 feet.

These waters, clouded by peat brought by rivers from the hills, are claimed to support the monster affectionately known as Nessie. Sightings have been recorded here since the Abbot of Iona's seventh century biography of St Columba described the holy man's encounter with an *aquatilis bestia* in this loch. In fact, most Highland lochs were traditionally believed by local people to harbour creatures of this sort. It is how-

ever at Loch Ness that scientific forays have been mounted and soundings and photographs taken – some quite difficult to challenge – but no conclusive evidence has been found.

Melrose Abbey

The superb ruin of Melrose Abbey on the Scottish Border bears witness to its former glory. The first Cistercian Abbey in Scotland, it was built for monks from Rieuvaulx in Yorkshire by David I in 1136. Little remains of the original building, which was repeatedly sacked during the Border wars, most notably in 1322 and 1385.

Most of today's remains are thought to date from 1385, although the abbey has lain in a state of decay since its last despoliation by the Earl of Hertford in 1545.

Even as a ruin the abbey's architecture, inspired by the late Decorated and early Perpendicular styles of the fourteenth century, shows a striking grace and majesty which is enriched as one draws closer by elaborate stonework, moulding and jointing of masonry, delicate carved foliage of bosses and capitals and images of saints, humans, animals and gargoyles. One of the most striking features is the superb window of five lights, with its intricate tracery, in the south transept. On the west wall of this transept two inscriptions refer to a master-mason John Morvo, the only known master-craftsman of the many who must have worked at Melrose, one of the finest buildings of its kind in the country.

Other commemorative inscriptions are to be found in the eight remaining chapels of the south nave aisle, which were the burial places of prominent families, although a thirteenth century stone set into the floor of the eighth chapel is inscribed (in Latin) 'Pray for the soul of Brother Peter, the Cellarer'. An embalmed heart in a silver casket, thought to be that of Robert the Bruce, is buried under the noble east window in the presbytery.

The presbytery has a fine vaulted ceiling, the bosses skilfully carved to represent figures of saints. The caps of the piers in the eastern part of the nave, ornamented by elaborate leaf motifs, show a fine example of the abbey's 'curly green' sculpture. The many surviving decorations, some disfigured, speak of wanton destruction and stoic rebuilding all in one breath. Among the many remaining sculptures of the hand-

some doorway to the south transept, a carved figure, looking upward, supporting a now-empty pedestal, holds a scroll inscribed 'Behold the Son of God'.

Perhaps the eloquent comment appears on a headstone in the churchyard, dated 1761, which ends,
'The earth builds on the earth castles and towers
The earth says to the earth all shall be ours'.

Neidpath Castle

This stronghold stands at the edge of a precipitous incline overlooking a narrow glen cut by the River Tweed. A typical thirteenth century Scottish peel tower, Neidpath was fortified in the fifteenth century and was improved in the sixteenth century by the second Earl of Tweedsdale, who cut a new entrance through the eleven-foot wall, installed a fine staircase, built stables and terraced the formidable slopes. The castle was later held against Cromwell's men who were stationed at Peebles, which is now a pleasant country town set amid wooded hills a few miles down-river. Neidpath was the last castle of the Scottish resistance to capitulate; cannon marks pit the walls.

The castle changed ownership and in the nineteenth century the fourth Earl of Queensbury (known as 'Old Q') became an absentee landlord. The slopes were stripped of their fine oaks, the terraces were grazed by sheep, thorn and under-growth sprang up. The castle was left to decay, as Wordsworth protested in a strongly-worded poem, 'beggared and outraged'.

Neidpath is now cared for by its present owner, the Earl of Wemyss and March. Recently restored, the castle serves as a stern reminder of the past whilst the river, flowing between grassy banks and woodland, affords peaceful picnicking sites. Visitors climbing the slopes enter the castle courtyard through an arched portal. Set into the keystone is a goat's head on a coronet, emblem of the Hays of Yester who became the Earls of Tweedsdale; a bunch of strawberries (fraises) beneath indicates the castle's change of ownership through the female line when the daughter of the last of the Frasers who owned Neidpath, married into the Yester family.

The second Earl's main entrance is ascended by a graceful, curved flight of steps and it leads straight into the first floor, so steep is the slope on which the castle stands. The interior is typical of

MELROSE ABBEY
Overleaf: In the Middle Ages Melrose—built by the Cistercian Order—was one of the richest abbeys in Scotland. Its situation in the Border country, however, made it prey to periodic violence, and after it was sacked by the English in 1545 it fell into decay.

NEIDPATH CASTLE
Picturesquely sited beside the River Tweed, Neidpath Castle has recently been restored, after several centuries of decay. In 1650, it was besieged by Cromwell, but did not surrender. Its now-peaceful grounds are well-suited to picnicking.

the early L-shaped Scottish forts. A room leading off the entrance leads to the dungeon, the second floor is taken up with the Great Hall, which still retains its seventeenth century panelling, and the third floor contains two bedrooms, both still habitable. The older, east side of the building, however, is without a roof; the rooms without floors.

Oban

Surrounded by islands, mountains and water, and backed by its own green slopes, Oban is an attractive and popular resort. From the curved Corran Esplanade, or from the breathtaking Pulpit Hill, one can look across a bay studded with sails to the island of Kerrera, which protects Oban Harbour. Beyond the Firth of Lorne lies the island of Mull, which shelters the mainland from Atlantic depressions. Distant peaks inland afford protection from easterly and northerly winds so that the climate is gentle, the water warm and the foliage lush, with many varieties of exotic and unexpected shrubs.

Oban is an interesting little town. George Street is the main street, underneath which prehistoric caves are known to exist. On a hill behind the town, dominating the skyline, is MacCaig's Tower, a late-Victorian folly in the form of a colosseum. In the harbour, seals sometimes appear among the steamers, fishing boats and pleasure craft. Part of Oban's charm is that while it provides excellent facilities for visitors, the town's livestock market, fishing fleet, distillery, tweed mill and glassware factory flourish all the year round. In June it is the scene of the Gaelic Mod, a two week festival of song, music and poetry.

Oban in Gaelic means 'little bay', and Corran means 'curved shore'. South Pier, where fish auctions are held, and Railway Pier look across the bay to the Corran Esplanade lined with Victorian hotels, at the northern end of the town. There is a small museum which displays Stone Age relics found in the caves, and in the 1960s complex, Corran Halls, Scottish dancing and other entertainments are held. Further along the Esplanade is the Roman Catholic Cathedral, St Columba, built in 1922. The walk continues past the War Memorial, beside which is the pillar-like Dog Stone where the mythical Gaelic hero Fingal tied his dog Bran; past the romantic Donollie Castle, a twelfth century, ivy-clad ruin, and finally one arrives at the seaside pleasures of Ganavan Sands.

The Isle of Skye

The most romantic and for many the loveliest of the Hebridean Isles, Skye is forever associated with the story of Flora Macdonald and 'Bonnie Prince Charlie', whom she helped escape to the island. However it is not only this colourful excursion into British history that has attracted visitors since the days of Dr Johnson (who met Flora Macdonald) and of Sir Walter Scott, and the travel-conscious Victorians. It is the island's dominating mountain scenery, its wild life and its poetic, almost mystic beauty.

Like the mainland close by, Skye is deeply indented with sea lochs which give it a wildly irregular outline of broad peninsula reaching in all directions from a small inland area. To the sixteenth century Irish, Skye was known as the Winged Island (possibly because of its shape) and for the Norsemen who settled it, the Isle of Cloud (possibly because of its mists). It is 50 miles long, between four and 24 miles wide, and no point is further than five miles from the sea.

From the touring resort of Broadford on the south-east shore of the central region, one can reach Sligachan, touring centre for the western Cuillin Hills, At the foot of these mountains lies the lonely Loch Coruisk, at its best when viewed from the peak of Drumhain.

Cuillin's misty peaks, some reaching over 3000 feet, make testing sport for experienced mountaineers. The mountain roads and passes allow scramblers to reach grassy deep valleys, called 'corries', streams, pools and waterfalls.

All 23 of Cuillin's black gabbro peaks can be seen across Loch Slapin from Sleat, Skye's south wing – from places such as Ord or Torvaig, where the ruins of Dunscaith Castle rise from red sands on Sleat's lonely west shore.

On Sleat's east coast, at Isleoronsay, are trees, lush hedgerows and whitewashed crofts.

From the pretty main town, Portree, the east coast road going north enters the freakish geological landscape of Trotternish. The road passes fantastic greyish pinnacles, steep jagged black cliffs, corries of rich grass and lochs. Most notable is the Quiraing, 'the pillared stronghold', a group of towers where cattle were driven during forays, and which also houses a large amphitheatre. Before reaching the Quiraing the road passes the landmark pinnacle, the Old Man of Storr, and then the pleated strata of Kilt Rock cliffs. The coastal edge of the Quiraing slopes down

THE ISLE OF SKYE
Overleaf: This Hebridean island is as lovely and romantic as its name suggests. Historically, it is famous as the island to which 'Bonnie Prince Charlie' escaped in 1745, aided by Flora Macdonald. Geographically it is of interest for its caves (which afforded shelter to the Prince), its jagged peaks and deep valleys, and its many pools and waterfalls.

OBAN
Right: Fishing boats represent one of Oban's main industries—the others being distilling, glass-making and weaving. The colosseum in the distance is a late-Victorian folly known as MacCaig's Tower. Oban's protected location gives it a relatively warm climate, one reason for its popularity. Another attraction is its annual festival of Gaelic music and poetry.

to pastures and crofts on Staffin Bay.

Just north of the Quiraing is Flodigarry, where the celebrated Flora Macdonald lived early in her marriage. From there the moorland road follows round the northern extreme of Trotternish, past the ruins of Duntulm Castle to Kilmuir, Flora Macdonald's burial place, where there is a craft museum. Here, and on all parts of Skye, are caves where it is said the prince hid and was brought provisions, while there was a £30,000 price on his head.

Green pastures around Uig Bay look across Loch Snizort to Vaternish, the central north wing of Skye. Trumpan, on the west shore, still has the ruins of a church where in 1578 the local population of Macleods was burned at prayer on a punitive raid by Macdonalds from Uist. But the Macdonalds on returning to their boats were then slaughtered by the rest of the Macleod clan mustered from Dunvegan Castle, some miles south. The castle, for 700 years occupied by Macleods and part of which is now open to the public, stands on a beautiful, wooded shore. A frail silk cloth from the Middle East, the Fairy Flag, which was the talisman invoked during the revenge at Trumpan, is displayed in a glass case.

St Andrews

On the Fife coast the ancient town of St Andrews is dominated by the remnants of Scotland's largest-ever cathedral. The stark façades overlook the harbour whose main pier, rebuilt in the seventeenth century, incorporates stone from the ruin. To this site were brought relics of St Andrew in the eighth century, when the See of Scotland was founded here, and when Scotland adopted her patron saint. Scotland's first university was founded here in 1411; and St Andrews is acknowledged as golf capital of the world. A ruined castle, with awful bottle dungeon, broods on a rocky bluff jutting into the sea. From there, the Scores leads west to the Royal and Ancient Golf Club (the 'R and A'). The university buildings, town hall and church, the many fine buildings with their 'riggs', or long gardens, and a network of ancient wynds interweave between South Street, Market Street and North Street which fan westward from the cathedral ruin.

South Street is entered by the restored sixteenth century West Port, and it ends at the Pends, the fourteenth century remains of an arched entrance gateway to the Cathedral's precincts. Little is left of the cathedral apart from

the west bell tower and the east front, separated by a span of some 391 feet. Begun in 1161, the building took over 150 years to build, saw the marriage of Mary of Guise to James V, and continued to flourish until its desecration 21 years later by John Knox and his reformers, whose work was centred around the town.

The college buildings are situated around North Street and South Street. The oldest is the sixteenth century tower of the church of St Salvator, but St Mary's, now a theological college, is thought to be most beautiful. An important collection of ancient manuscripts is preserved in the library, which occupies two sides of the quadrangle where there is a thorn tree planted by Mary, Queen of Scots. The renovated town hall next door holds the eleventh-century Burgh Charter granted by Malcolm Canmore; less peaceably, the headsman's axe is displayed. A fine mosaic was the gift of Polish soldiers garrisoned here during World War II.

A silver Book of Remembrance dating from that time is to be found opposite in Holy Trinity Church, remodelled to its original fifteenth century form in 1906. Although a Presbyterian church, Holy Trinity's south transept holds a marble statue of the Episcopalian Archbishop Sharp, murdered by Covenanters in 1679. Among many other interesting relics and memorials is a tablet to the famous golfer, Old Tom Morris, on the west wall.

The hallowed golf courses, of which the Old is most venerated (it is five centuries old), stand by the sea at the north-west of the promontory on which St Andrews stands. The Old Course's most testing stretches are the natural sand bunkers, the Swilcan Burn, and the sea winds which spring up to veer, bluster and confuse.

Other recreational amenities are provided in two miles of sandy beach, and in Craigton Park two miles south, which is based around a mansion house and estate, and known as the Family Playground.

Stirling Castle

Stirling is Scotland's most noble castle. It is a fortress in the Forth Valley occupying a position of supreme strategic importance, high on a cliff, guarding the passage to the north of Scotland. It was one of the four royal residences; fifteenth century parliaments met in James III's Great Hall, in 1543 the infant Mary,

ST. ANDREWS
Overleaf: The university town of St. Andrews has much to offer the visitor— medieval buildings, including a ruined castle, a fine beach with swimming —for the hardy—in the North Sea, and one of the world's great golf courses.

STIRLING CASTLE
Right: Mary, Queen of Scots was crowned in this strong royal residence. Built in the fifteenth and sixteenth centuries, it is an early example of Scottish Renaissance architecture. It stands on the site of an earlier fortress which, during the endless wars between the English and Scots, changed hands frequently. The existing castle has elaborately carved facades and impressive royal apartments.

Queen of Scots was crowned here and, in 1566, her two-month-old son, James, soon to be crowned king, was baptized here; but it is as a castle stronghold that Stirling holds its place in history. Of its many battles, occupations and sieges, the three-month stand against Edward I's siege of 1303, his 11-year occupation and the resulting Battle of Bannockburn must rank as one of the castle's most notable episodes.

Nothing remains of the castle as it was then. The earliest surviving structures are James III's fifteenth century 'foirface', the remains of a great Gatehouse with curtain walls and flanking towers, through which visitors pass to the Parade. Preceding this inner entry is the formidable gateway of an early eighteenth century arched entrance through a massive curtain wall, flanked by the Queen Anne Battery on the west, and the Overport on the east.

Past these defences, the main buildings consist of James V's Palace, the Great Hall and the Chapel Royal built by James VI, grouped around an inner square. The Hall and the Chapel were used as a garrison and armoury in the eighteenth century, and their interiors stripped. The palace retains its apartments, facing on to a small square called the Lion's Den, where reputedly the royal animals were kept. The outer façades are of considerable charm and interest as some of the earliest examples of Scottish classic Renaissance architecture. They are decorated with a profusion of exuberant stone carvings in curved recessed arches, between generous rounded windows. Among the cherubs' heads, gargoyles, figures of nude boys, reclining females and groups of courtiers is a figure on the north façade thought to represent James V as the 'guidman o' Ballangeich', a disguise, it is said, he adopted so that he might study the everyday living conditions of his subjects.

The Royal Apartments, on the 'Belle Etage', the first floor, retain only their fine fireplaces, as generously carved as the outer façades, and some formidable oak doors.

The old town of Stirling, like Edinburgh, dates from the sixteenth to the eighteenth centuries and is grouped along a steep approach to the castle. The lower town of Stirling, however, is predominantly Victorian.

Stirling was chosen as the site for Scotland's fifth university, the first new university to be founded in Scotland for 400 years.

Traquair House

The oldest inhabited house in Scotland, Traquair House has legends and history to match. It is a predominantly seventeenth century mansion, built in French château style and based around its north-east tower, which is 1000 years old.

Traquair's beautiful wooded grounds are imbued with a sense of the past, and they have been enlivened by the conversion of ancient barns and byres into workshops for local jewellers, potters, weavers and other craft workers; the 200-year-old brewhouse is licensed to provide the unique Traquair Ale. A cottage tearoom and gift shop make a pleasant addition to the grounds, and a mile or so away the confluence of two rivers, Quair Water and the Tweed, offers places for picnics and walks.

Traquair is occupied and cared for by descendants of the Stuarts of Traquair. Its gates are welcomingly open but the imposing heraldic gateway, flanked by massive stone bears, has remained closed since Prince Charles Edward's visit in 1746 and will remain so until a Stuart next occupies the Scottish throne. In the house itself, treasures and relics dating back over six centuries also speak of Traquair's past.

The house is said to have been visited by 27 Scots or English kings and queens, and an 'Amen' glass engraved with a toast to Prince Charlie recalls the visit of that would-be king. A cradle in one of the bedrooms makes a touching reminder of Mary, Queen of Scots' visit in 1566 with her disaffected husband Henry Darnley and their baby. Other treasures include manuscripts, pictures and books, embroideries, silver and glass.

Perhaps best of all is the sense of continuity about this house which, with its relics, its priest's hole and its eighteenth century library, must be as exciting to live in as it is to visit.

The Trossachs

So popular has the Trossachs become that the name now encompasses a far greater region, including the Queen Elizabeth Park; but the true Trossachs is a pass linking Loch Katrine, to the west, with the smaller, wooded Loch Achray. This loch in turn is connected by two miles of river to Loch Vennachar. A road runs from Callender, the prototype for the television series *Dr Finlay's Casebook*, along the north shores of both

lochs, turning southward around the western point of Loch Achray up a steep and scenically-exciting route to the popular centre Aberfoyle.

At this turn the road diverges and continues through the Trossachs, a stony pass cutting between the mountains Ben Venue to the south-west and Ben A'an to the north-east. The slopes are a tangle of oak, beech, myrtle, juniper and other wild shrubs, and the pass is justly famed for its wild beauty; wild, but never harsh. The road ends at the head of Loch Katrine, which is open to walkers but not to cars, since it is now a water reservoir.

Sir Walter Scott popularized the Trossachs by his use of the area round Loch Katrine in his narrative poem *The Lady of the Lake*, and today the steamer *Sir Walter Scott* makes daily trips, passing Ellen's Island at the east end; Ellen being the Lady, Loch Katrine the Lake. The region also forms the background for Scott's novel about the romantic Robin Hood figure, the Macgregor bandit Rob Roy, whose clan had the run of the mountains and glens all round, extending west to Loch Lomond.

A good view of Loch Katrine set in its rugged mountains can be gained from the twin-peaked Ben Venue. A pass leads southwards toward the mountain from the head of Loch Achray and then through the higher ground of Bealach nam Bo, or Pass of the Cattle (rustled by the Macgregors and Rob Roy). Far below is a complex of caverns known as the Goblins', or Satyrs', Caves. On the northern shore of Loch Achray is the charming village of Brig o'Turk, lying at the steep mouth of Glan Finglas which cuts past Ben A'an to the loch. Scattered white houses stand at varying heights along the mouth of the glen. In the heather-covered graveyard of the village church are ancient stones bearing the names of Stewarts, and of Macgregors. Further north along the glen, where the road ends at another, smaller reservoir, is the Brig o' Turk Inn, once the home of the fattest woman in the kingdom, Muckle Kate Ferguson, weighing 24 stone.

To the west of Loch Achray is the splendid, Gothic-style Trossachs Hotel, built to accommodate the sightseers of Victorian times.

For Your Information

Addresses and telephone numbers (local dialling codes in brackets)

ENGLAND

British Tourist Authority, 64 St James's Street, London
SW1 01–629 9191
English Tourist Board, 4 Grosvenor Gardens, London SW1
01–730 3400
Alum Bay and Needles (Isle of Wight)
Isle of Wight Tourist Board, Yarmouth (0983) 760015
Arundel Castle (Sussex)
Arundel Castle, Arundel (0903) 882 73
Arundel Tourist Information Centre, 61 High Street,
Arundel (0903) 882268
Bath Spa (Avon)
Bath Information Centre, 8 Abbey Church Yard, Bath
(0225) 62831 and 60521
Blackpool (Lancashire)
Blackpool Information and Accommodation Bureau, The
Promenade, Blackpool (0253) 21623
The Royal Pavilion, Brighton (Sussex)
Brighton Tourist Information Centres, Marlborough House,
54 Old Steine, Brighton (0273) 23755
Sea Front, Kings Road (0273) 26450 (summer only)
Canterbury Cathedral (Kent)
Canterbury Cathedral Chapter Office, 8 The Precincts,
Canterbury (0227) 63135
Canterbury Tourist Information Centre, 22 St Peter's
Street (0227) 66567
Cheddar Gorge (Avon)
Cheddar Caves, Cheddar (0934) 742343
Chester : The Rows (Cheshire)
Chester Heritage Centre, St Michael's Church, Bridge
Street, Chester (0223) 317948
Chester Tourist Information Centre, Town Hall (0223)
40144 ext 2111 and 49026 (evenings and weekends)
Dartmoor (Devon)
Dartmoor National Park, Bovey Tracey (0626) 832093
Fishbourne Roman Palace (Sussex) Chichester
(0243) 785859
Flatford Mill (Suffolk)
Flatford Mill Centre, Colchester (0206) 298283
Hampton Court Palace (Greater London)
Information 01–977 8441
The Lake District (Cumbria)
Cumbria Tourist Board, Ellerthwaite, Windermere
(096 62) 4444
Windermere Tourist Information Centres, Victoria Street,
Windermere (096 62) 4561 (summer only)
Bowness Bay (096 62) 2244 ext 43 and 2895
Leeds Castle (Kent)
Leeds Castle Foundation, Visitors' Enquiries,
Hollingbourne (062 780) 456
Salisbury Cathedral (Wiltshire)
Tourist Information Centres, 10 Endless Street, Salisbury
(0722) 4956
Fisherton Place (0772) 4432
**Shakespeare's Birthplace and Anne Hathaway's
Cottage (Warwickshire)**
Stratford-upon-Avon Tourist Information Centre, Judith
Shakespeare House, 1 High Street, Stratford-upon-Avon
(0789) 293127
King Arthur's Castle, Tintagel (Cornwall)
Tintagel (084 04) 328
Windsor Castle (Berkshire)
Chapter Clerk, Windsor Castle, Windsor (95) 65538
York Minster (Yorkshire)
Information Officer, York Minster (0904) 24426
Tour Information Centre, De Grey Rooms, Exhibition
Square, York (0904) 217567

WALES

The Brecon Beacons (South Wales)
The Brecon Beacons National Park, 7 Glamorgan Street,
Brecon (0874) 2763
The Brecon Beacons Mountain Centre, near Libanus
(0874) 3366
Caernarvon (Gwynedd)
Superintendent of Works Office and Castle, Caernarvon
(0286) 3094
Wales Tourist Office, Slate Quay (0286) 2232 (Easter-
September)
Portmeirion (Gwynedd)
Portmeirion Shops, Penrhyndeudraeth (0766) 770453
Tenby (Dyfed)
Museum, Castle Hill, Tenby (0834) 2809
Tourist Information Bureau, The Croft, Tenby (0834) 2404
Snowdonia (Gwynedd)
National Park Office, Penrhyndeudraeth (0766) 770702

LONDON

London Tourist Board, 26 Grosvenor Gardens SW1
01–730 0791
The British Museum (WC1) 01–636 1555
National Gallery, Trafalgar Square WC2 01–839 3321
Tate Gallery, Millbank SW1 01–821 1313
Buckingham Palace (SW1) 01–930 4832
**Camden Lock and Little Venice on Regent's Canal
(NW1/W2)**
London Zoo, Regent's Park NW1 01–586 2765
Chelsea (SW3)
Royal Hospital Chelsea Museum 01–730 0161
National Army Museum, Royal Hospital Road
01–730 0717
Fleet Street (EC4)
City of London Information Centre, St Paul's Churchyard
01–606 3030
Greenwich (SE10)
National Maritime Museum, Romney Road 01–858 4422
Greenwich Information Bureau, King William Walk,
Cutty Sark Gardens 01–858 6376
Art and Science in South Kensington (SW7)
British Museum (Natural History), Cromwell Road
01–589 6323
Science Museum, Exhibition Road 01–589 3456
Victoria and Albert Museum, Exhibition Road 01–589 6371
**Parliament Square and the Houses of Parliament
(SW1)**
House of Commons, General Information 01–219 3000
House of Lords, Parliamentary Information 01–219
3107/5428
St Paul's Cathedral (EC4)
City of London Information Centre, St Paul's Churchyard
01–606 3030
South Bank (SE1)
Royal Festival Hall, Queen Elizabeth Hall, Purcell Room,
Belvedere Road 01–928 3002
National Film Theatre 01–928 3232
Street Markets
Leadenhall Market, Gracechurch Street EC3
Bermondsey Antique Market, 25 Long Lane SE1
01–407 4635
Portobello Antiques Market, 165 Portobello Road W11
01–229 4010

Tower Bridge (SE1)
Superintendent Engineer's Office 01–407 0922/2129
The Tower of London (EC3) 01–709 0765
Waterside Pubs Down-River
The Anchor Inn, 1 Bankside SE1 01–407 1577
01–407 3003 (Restaurant)
The George Inn, 77 Borough High Street, Southwark SE1
01–407 2056
The Angel, Rotherhithe Street SE16
The Mayflower, 117 Rotherhithe Street SE16
01–237 1898/4088 (Restaurant)
The Prospect of Whitby, 57 Wapping Wall E1
01–481 1095/1317
The Trafalgar Tavern, Park Row SE10 01–858 2507
The Cutty Sark Restaurant and Tavern, Lassell Street
SE10 01–858 3146
Westminster Abbey (SW1) 01–222 1051

IRELAND

Northern Ireland Tourist Board, River House, 48-52 High
Street, Belfast (0232) 46609
Tourist Office (Irish), 53 Castle Street, Belfast (0232) 27888
Tourist Services Ireland, 29 Wating Street, Belfast
(0232) 22454
Irish Tourist Board—Board Failte, P.O. Box 273, Dublin 8
(Postal Enquiries)
Irish Tourist Office, Ireland House, 150 New Bond Street,
London W1 01–493 3201
Bantry House and Bay (County Cork, Eire)
Tourist Information Office, Bantry (021) 229 (June-
September)
Belfast (County Antrim, Northern Ireland)
Tourist Information Centre, River House, 48-52 High
Street, Belfast (0232) 46609
**Carrickfergus Castle (County Antrim, Northern
Ireland)**
Carrickfergus (0906) 62273
Dublin (County Dublin, Eire)
Tourist Information Office, 51 Dawson Street, Dublin 1
(01) 747733
Kerry (County Kerry, Eire)
Tourist Information Office, Town Hall, Killarney
(064) 31633

SCOTLAND

Scottish Tourist Board, 5 Pall Mall East, SW1 01–930 8661
Scottish Tourist Board, 5 Waverly Bridge, Edinburgh
(031) 332 2433
Braemar (Aberdeenshire)
Braemar Castle (033 83) 219
Tourist Information Centre, Kindrochit Castle, Braemar
(May-October) (033 83) 600
Culzean Castle and Country Park (Ayrshire)
All Enquiries and Reservations, Kirkoswald (065 56) 269
Edinburgh Castle (Midlothian)
Scottish United Services Museum, Crown Square,
The Castle
Edinburgh Tourist Information Centre, 5 Waverly Bridge,
Edinburgh (031) 226 6591
Fort William and Ben Nevis (Invernesshire)
General Enquiries, Fort William (0397) 3581
Holyrood Abbey and Palace (Edinburgh)
Holyrood Palace, Department of the Environment/
Property Services Agency, Sergeant Warder
(031) 556 0252
Inveraray Castle (Argyllshire)
Chamberlain of Argyll, Inveraray (0499) 2203
Inveraray Tourist Board, Inveraray (0499) 2063
Loch Ness (Invernesshire)
Inverness, Loch Ness and Nairn Information Centre,
Nairn Bus Station, King Street, Nairn (0667) 52753
(mid-May to mid-September)
Melrose Abbey (Roxburghshire)
Priorwood Information Centre, near Abbey Melrose
(085 682) 2555 (summer only)
The Isle of Skye (Invernesshire)
Broadford Information Centre, Broadford (047 12) 361/463
St Andrews (Fifeshire)
Tourist Information Centre, South Street, St Andrews
(0334) 2021
Stirling Castle (Stirlingshire)
Department of the Environment, Stirling (0786) 62421
Stirling Tourist Information Centre, Dumbarton Road,
Stirling (0786) 5019
Information Centre, Bannockburn (0786) 814026 (March-
September)
Traquair House (Peeblesshire)
General Enquiries, Shop and Traquair Ale, Innerleithen
(0896) 323
The Trossachs (Perthshire)
Tour Information Office, Glasgow District Council,
George Square (041) 221 6136/7 or 7371/2

SCOTLAND

Braemar

St Andrews

Edinburgh Castle
and Holyrood

Border Abbeys
and Castles

Tweed

Loch
Ness

Inveraray The
Castle Trossachs

Stirling
Castle

Fort
William

Ben
Nevis

Oban

Loch
Lomond

The Isle
of Skye

Giant's

N